"Barbara Slate's new and highly original book shines forth a path, step by step, that navigates the reader to a better understanding of one's self and the creative process."

George Braziller

"Attention, hopeful comics writers: Barbara Slate has given you a helping hand with *YOU CAN DO A GRAPHIC NOVEL*, a colorful, funny, and user-friendly way to attain your goal. With Slate's perfect combination of brightly illustrated tips and no-nonsense rules, you'll find that YOU CAN DO A GRAPHIC NOVEL!"

Trina Robbins
Comics Creator and Historian,
Author of *A Century of Women Cartoonists*

"Barbara Slate's exciting new book brings to life, in a wonderful, colorful format her careful, yet joyful, instructive and imaginative method of teaching the graphic novel that I experienced during her classes at our local library."

Jeanne Leonard
Director of Children's Programs,
Claverack Library, NY

"Working side-by-side with Barbara was one of the best career choices I have ever made. Not only did I get a chance to work on comics and graphic novels, but I learned as much from her as I did in my four years at art school! I still hear her voice every time I sit down at my drawing table. Establishing shots, push pull, make it fun … And now that I am teaching, I'm quoting her more than ever!!!"

Jerry Craft
Creator of *Mama's Boyz*
Syndicated by King Features

YOU CAN DO A GRAPHIC NOVEL

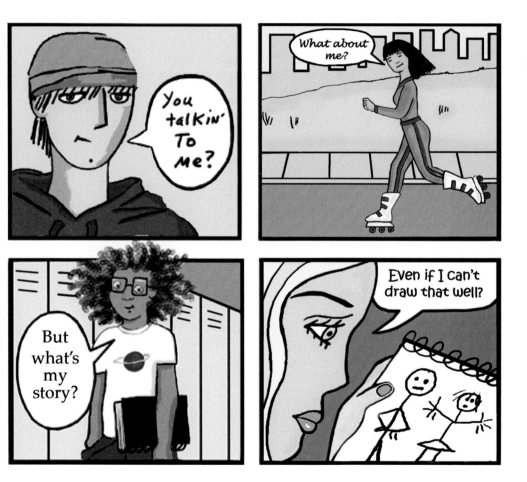

BARBARA SLATE

You Can Do a

Graphic Novel

BARBARA SLATE

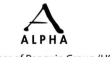

ALPHA

A member of Penguin Group (USA) Inc.

ALPHA BOOKS

Published by the Penguin Group

Penguin Group (USA) Inc., 375 Hudson Street, New York, New York 10014, USA

Penguin Group (Canada), 90 Eglinton Avenue East, Suite 700, Toronto, Ontario M4P 2Y3, Canada (a division of Pearson Penguin Canada Inc.)

Penguin Books Ltd., 80 Strand, London WC2R 0RL, England

Penguin Ireland, 25 St. Stephen's Green, Dublin 2, Ireland (a division of Penguin Books Ltd.)

Penguin Group (Australia), 250 Camberwell Road, Camberwell, Victoria 3124, Australia (a division of Pearson Australia Group Pty. Ltd.)

Penguin Books India Pvt. Ltd., 11 Community Centre, Panchsheel Park, New Delhi—110 017, India

Penguin Group (NZ), 67 Apollo Drive, Rosedale, North Shore, Auckland 1311, New Zealand (a division of Pearson New Zealand Ltd.)

Penguin Books (South Africa) (Pty.) Ltd., 24 Sturdee Avenue, Rosebank, Johannesburg 2196, South Africa

Penguin Books Ltd., Registered Offices: 80 Strand, London WC2R 0RL, England

International Standard Book Number: 978-1-59257-955-6
Library of Congress Catalog Card Number: 2009930703

12 11 10   8 7 6 5 4 3 2 1

Interpretation of the printing code: The rightmost number of the first series of numbers is the year of the book's printing; the rightmost number of the second series of numbers is the number of the book's printing. For example, a printing code of 10-1 shows that the first printing occurred in 2010.

Printed in the United States of America

Note: This publication contains the opinions and ideas of its author. It is intended to provide helpful and informative material on the subject matter covered. It is sold with the understanding that the author and publisher are not engaged in rendering professional services in the book. If the reader requires personal assistance or advice, a competent professional should be consulted.

The author and publisher specifically disclaim any responsibility for any liability, loss, or risk, personal or otherwise, which is incurred as a consequence, directly or indirectly, of the use and application of any of the contents of this book.

Trademarks: All terms mentioned in this book that are known to be or are suspected of being trademarks or service marks have been appropriately capitalized. Alpha Books and Penguin Group (USA) Inc. cannot attest to the accuracy of this information. Use of a term in this book should not be regarded as affecting the validity of any trademark or service mark.

Most Alpha books are available at special quantity discounts for bulk purchases for sales promotions, premiums, fund-raising, or educational use. Special books, or book excerpts, can also be created to fit specific needs.

For details, write: Special Markets, Alpha Books, 375 Hudson Street, New York, NY 10014.

This book is dedicated to
all my students, who taught me well.

Contents

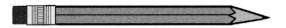

Thank you

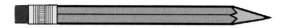

My two fan boys, Richard Minsky and Richard C. Levy, both born January 7, 1947 … my lucky day.

Jenette Kahn, president of DC Comics, who gave me my first big break.

Tom DeFalco, editor-in-chief of Marvel Comics, who gave me my second, third, fourth, and fifth breaks.

Dick Giordano and Paul Levitz who taught me how to plot.

Stan Goldberg, Dan DeCarlo, Jane Gennaro, Bert Stern, Pat Gorman, George Braziller, Inez Geller, and Jerry Craft for inspiring me.

Karen Berger, Joe Orlando, Bobby Chase, Sid Jacobson, Victor Gorelick, Parry Teasdale, editors who helped make me look good.

Hildy Mesnik, my dear friend and the editor who guided this book throughout its development.

Mike Sanders, who said "yes" and was there 24/7, Dawn Werk, Megan Douglass, Bill Thomas, Laura Caddell, the prodigious Pearson team who helped form, shape, produce, market, and promote this book.

Nancy Hoag, who got me started teaching at the Claverack Library in upstate NY.

My high school art teacher, Mr. Firestone, who said, "Draw what you see, not what you think you see."

My family, Charlie and Pearl Slate, Sheryl and Bettie C. Levy, Jeffrey Slate, and Emily Masters.

Samantha Slate, my daughter and art assistant.

Jean Leonard, Sally Alderdice, Jenny Post, Joan Steiner from the Claverack Library

Greta Boeringer, Hudson Area Association Library

Carol Roberts, Troy Public Library

Becky Klein, Chatham Library

Tom Daily & Melinda Georgeson, Norman Rockwell Museum

Barbara Flach, Greenville Public Library

Debby Cuthbert, Lenox Library

Julie H. Johnson, Alanna Almstead, Kinderhook Library

Gwenn Mayers, Susan Merrett, Parker School

Claire Pollart, Berkshire Country Day School

Gayil Greene, Joe Mello, Roselle Grubin, Steven Zurrow, Gini Peterson, Judy and Marty Shepard, Donna and Jim Campion, Pat and Bernie Goldstein, Richard and Ronnie Grosbard, Marion Wolberg Weiss, Arlene Bujese, Helen Silverman, Phyllis Braff, Dr. John Gray, Dr. Stephen Krizar, Rose Slivka, and last but not least, Sparky.

Foreword

I used to think Barbara Slate was crazy. Don't get me wrong! That's a pretty common characteristic for a lot of the writers and artists who spend their lives producing comics and graphic novels. As both a talented writer and an exceptional artist, poor Barbara never had a chance. She was always prone to the weird and wacky.

Barbara started down her road to ruin by creating and producing a series of feminist greeting cards that starred a character called Ms. Liz. Ms. Liz later went on to appear in a comic strip that was published in *Cosmopolitan* and in animated segments on the *Today Show*. While working on this material, Barbara discovered that she had a real talent for graphic storytelling. She started writing and drawing comic books like *Angel Love*, *Sweet XVI*, Disney's *Beauty and the Beast*, Mattel's *Barbie,* and Archie's *Betty & Veronica*. She also wrote and illustrated a pair of graphic novels called *Sex, Lies and Mutual Funds of the Yuppies from Hell* and *Son of Yuppies from Hell*. Quite an impressive resumé and I'm not even going to mention the series of Little Golden Books that she wrote. (Okay, maybe I *am*.)

A few years ago, Barbara Slate informed me that she had begun writing a newspaper column called, "You Can Do A Graphic Novel." Barbara has this wacky idea that she can teach everyone—from six to ninety-six (and even older)—how to produce comics and graphic novels. Barbara is convinced that she can show her readers how to take a simple idea and turn it into a visual scene. She also believes that she can explain how to tie these scenes together to form chapters, and use chapters to build a completed graphic novel.

Barbara thinks that anyone can learn how to write and draw a graphic novel. Anyone! Can you imagine such nonsense? She is so committed to this crazy idea that she has even been teaching a series of classes and workshops, and her students have already started producing some very promising material.

Yeah, I used to think Barbara Slate was crazy. After reading *You Can Do a Graphic Novel*, I'm not so sure about that, anymore.

—Tom DeFalco,
Editor-in-Chief, Marvel Comics (1995-2000)

MY STORY

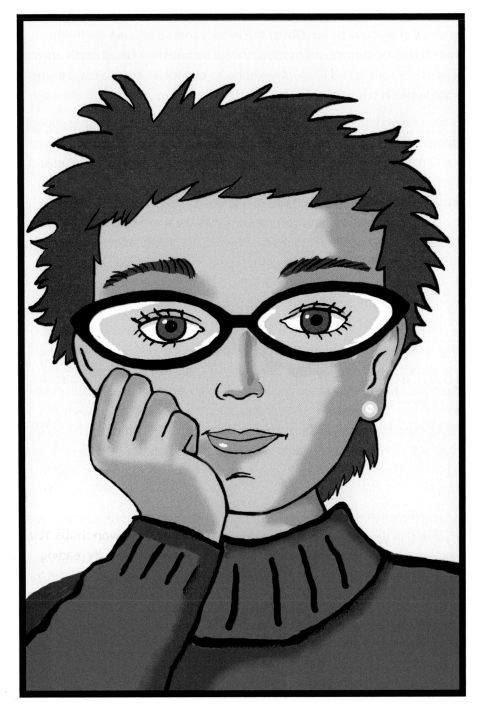

My life really began when I did my first comic book, *Angel Love,* for DC Comics. Since then I have written, drawn, or created more than 300 comic books and graphic novels for Marvel, DC, Disney, Harvey, and Archie Comics.

Three years ago, I was invited by my local library in upstate New York, to teach teenagers how to do a graphic novel. *I jumped at the chance!* Not only was it an opportunity for me to share my knowledge, but I needed to get away from my drawing board and interact with humans. And what better humans are there than teens?

I was scheduled to teach an hour and a half every Thursday evening for six weeks. Like any professional, I did my homework and made a lesson plan. The first week, I would talk about the creative process; the second week, character development; the third, plotline; the fourth would be about dialogue; the fifth, layout; and finally on the sixth week, I planned to talk about breaking into the business.

Fifteen students showed up for my graphic novel class. I was teaching for about five minutes when I realized that I had already gone through the creative process, character development, and how to plot. At that rate, I had another five minutes to go until I finished my entire lesson plan!

I looked around to see that all my students were sketching and doodling. That's when I got the big *AHA!* They didn't want somebody *talking* about how to do a graphic novel, they just wanted to *do* one.

And that's what we did. By following my students' lead, I was able to teach my entire lesson plan over the next six weeks. Everybody works at their own pace and has their own way of working. By observing the students' struggles, breakthroughs, and creative processes, I couldn't help getting inspired to write this book!

Since that first Thursday, I have taught many graphic novel workshops. *You Can Do a Graphic Novel* will assist you in your creative process. By reading this book, *you* will develop your characters and plot, write dialogue, get to know your creative process, create a layout, and learn about the comic book business, but it is up to *you* to *do* your graphic novel.

If you are about to do or are doing a graphic novel, then this book is for you. What are you waiting for? *Get to work!*

CHAPTER ONE

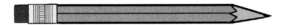

Your Story

You are unique. You have something to say that nobody else on this planet has to say. *Find it.* Search for your voice. What do *you* have to contribute? What do *you* have to say?

Every story has a
beginning, middle, end,
and twist.
The twist is the surprise ...
the unexpected.

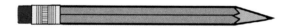

It can take many pages to write and draw your graphic novel but you should be able to tell your story in three sentences or less. Keep asking, *"What is my story?"* until you get it.

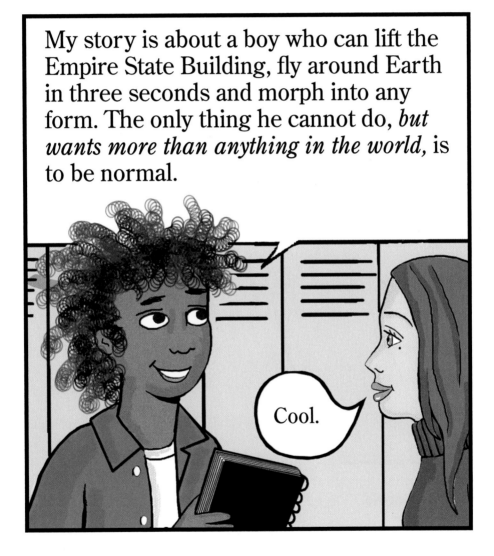

5

Your Successful Story

Most successful stories have a plan. Writers organize the events in their story according to the chart below:

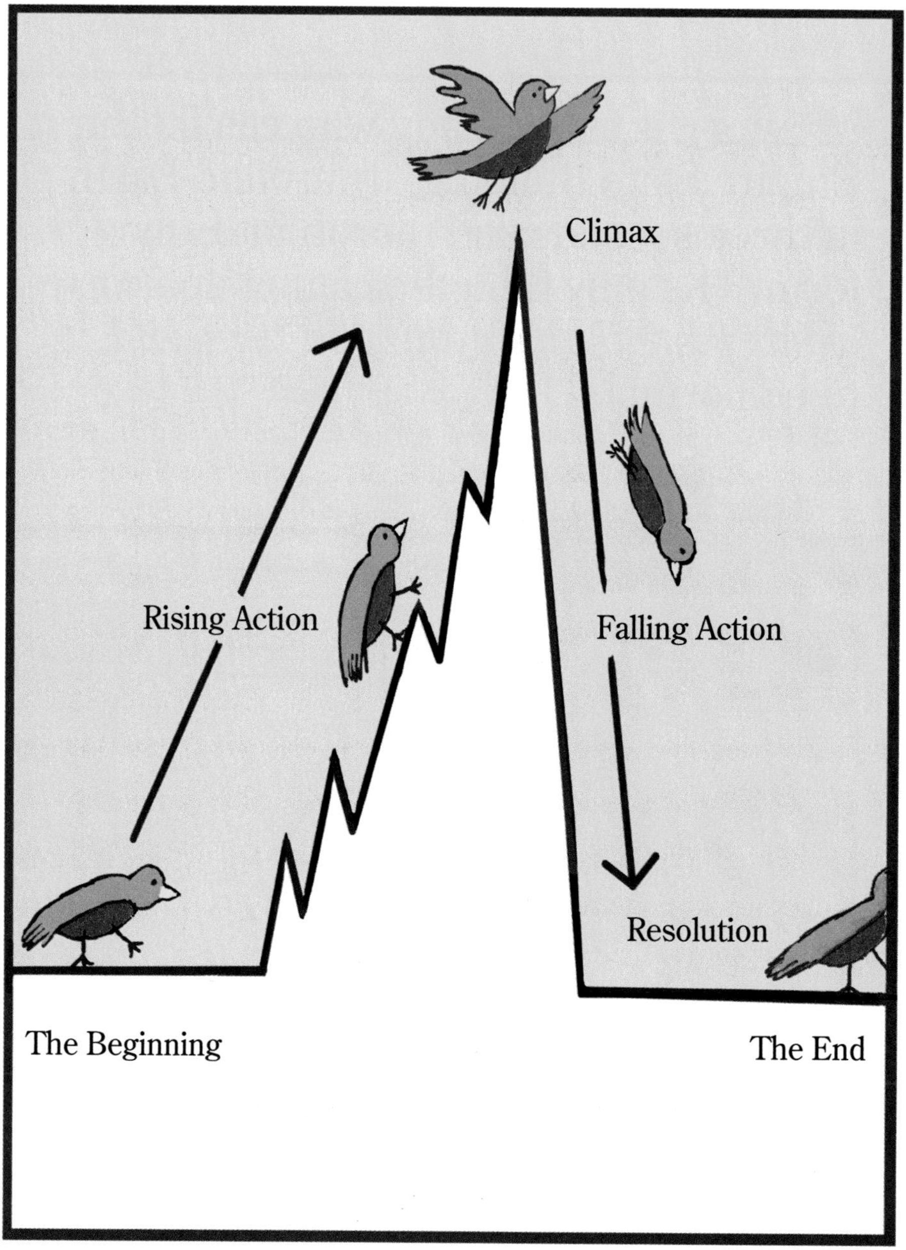

Climax

Rising Action

Falling Action

Resolution

The Beginning

The End

The Beginning

In graphic novels or comic books, the **splash page** is often the first page. Usually the splash page is one full page or sometimes even a double-page spread. Make *your* beginning grab the attention of your reader.

Rising Action

The central part of your story where the main conflict (problem) of your characters is developed. This is the build-up of your story. This is where the suspense, drama, or comedy (it can be all of them!) develop to create your successful story.

Climax

The moment of highest tension when the conflict comes to a boiling point. In the movie *The Wizard of Oz,* the climax occurs when we discover the Wizard is a fraud. Think of graphic novels or books that you have read or movies you've seen. Can you pick out the climax?

Falling Action

The part of the story when your main characters react to the climax. The falling action happens quickly. Think of your favorite movies and note when the climax occurs. Then notice how quickly the movie ends.

Resolution

The point when the conflict is successfully wrapped up.

The End

The final part of the story in which everything is made clear. Not all endings are happy. Some endings, especially in comic books, are "To Be Continued …"

Nobody likes a boring story.

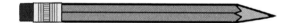

Did you ever go to a party where there is somebody telling a *really boring story* and somehow *you* got stuck being the *one and only* listener? You do not want to be rude but *come on!* You came to this party to have fun, not to listen to a boring story.

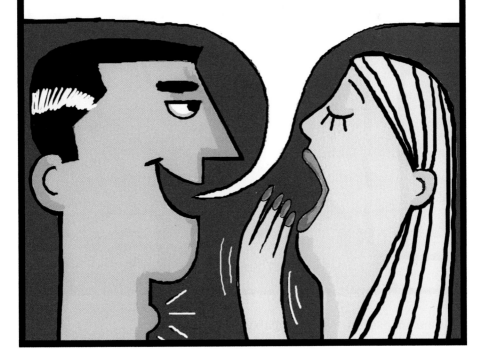

It was like raining and just my luck I lost my umbrella and then I ran outta gas and had to go shopping for my cats I have three cats their names are Molly Tiger and Lulu and just my luck the store was closed and then I got a ticket even though I wasn't going fast and I told the cop about my cats and by the way their names are Molly Tiger and Lulu and I needed to get home to feed them but the store was not open because I think it closed early even though most nights it is open late but just my luck—

One way to know if you are writing a dreary story is to ask …

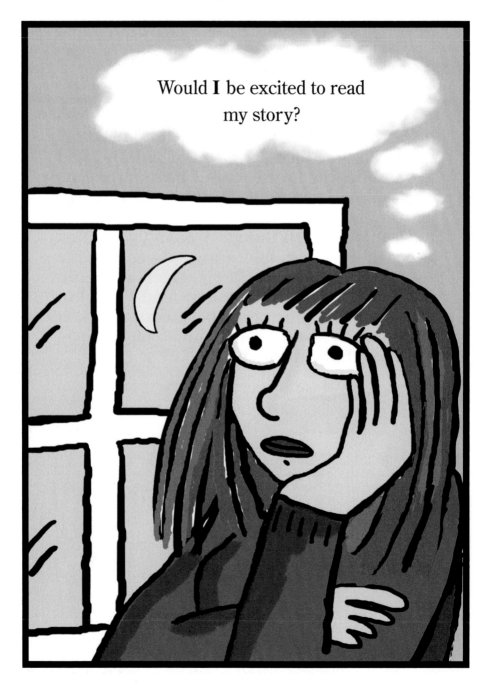

Would **I** be excited to read my story?

If *you* are not excited, then it probably is a boring story.

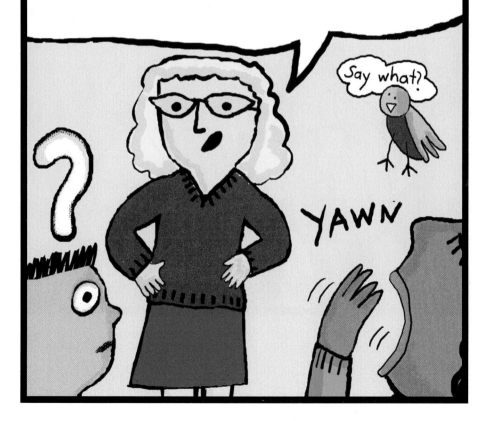

And finally, a third sign that your story might be boring is if your mother and girlfriend *both* love it.

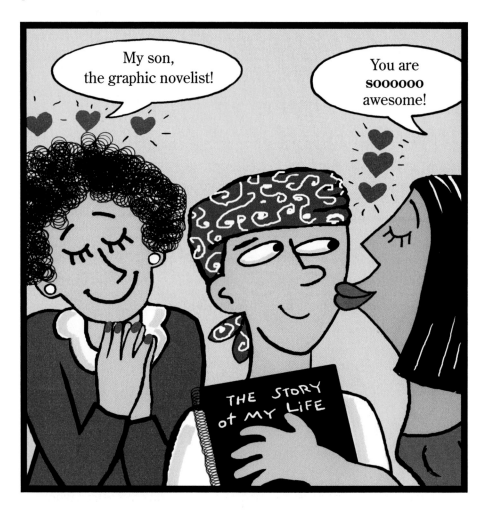

If you want a *truthful opinion*, show your pages to someone who doesn't adore you so much.

Feedback

When somebody reads your graphic novel and offers their opinion, that is called **feedback.** Not all feedback is going to be positive. Try not to get offended. Listen to what the person has to say. (When my editor gives me feedback, I like to write everything down and then go over the notes. If I have questions, I ask for more details.)

It may not be easy for you to let go of your work. You may feel exposed if your main character is you or part of you that nobody knew existed.

Show your pages to somebody you like and respect and who likes and respects you. You may find several people or just one person. It can be a friend, teacher, relative, editor, or your graphic novel partner.

Why feedback is important

※ Somebody might say something that sparks an idea you never thought of.

※ Somebody might say something you do not agree with, but later you get what they were saying.

※ Somebody might say something that is so stupid you wonder why you asked for their opinion in the first place.

Whether you like or don't like the critique, always thank the person who took the time to read your graphic novel.

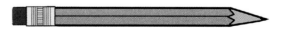

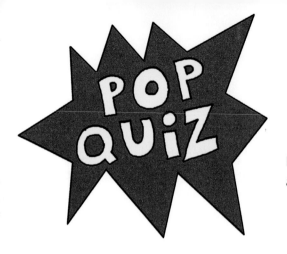

Here are two stories: one with a twist, and one without.

Choose the story with the twist.

1. My friend Rose was a great writer. One summer, Rose was busy meeting a deadline when she stopped to observe a spider weaving its web. She became fascinated with the industrious spider and took a picture of it. The next day, and every morning after that for a month, at 8 o' clock sharp, she carefully snapped a picture of the spider as it spun its wonderful web.

    At the end of 31 days, Rose was thrilled when she saw the fabulous photographs. Rose patiently pasted them in an album and called it "The Spider."

2. My friend Rose was a great writer. One summer, Rose was busy meeting a deadline when she stopped to observe a spider weaving its web. She became fascinated with the industrious spider and took a picture of it. The next day, and every morning after that for a month, at 8 o' clock sharp, she carefully snapped a picture of the spider as it spun its wonderful web.

    At the end of 31 days, Rose opened up her camera and much to her surprise discovered that she didn't have any film in it.

Answer: Story 2. In this true story, Rose didn't have pictures to paste in an album but she did have a great story to tell.

Your successful story has:

Protagonist

Your main character. The Protagonist is the person the reader cares about.

Antagonist

Adversary/opponent. Tries to stop the Protagonist from accomplishing his/her/its goals.

Conflict

The struggle between the Protagonist and the Antagonist.

Plot

The way the story unfolds and resolves.

Theme

The message at the core of your story.

Setting

The time and place of the story.

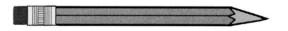

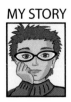

Write What You Know About

I was twenty when I moved to New York City from Harrisburg, Pennsylvania with my portfolio and fifty dollars in my pocket. As I rode the Greyhound bus, I remember thinking …

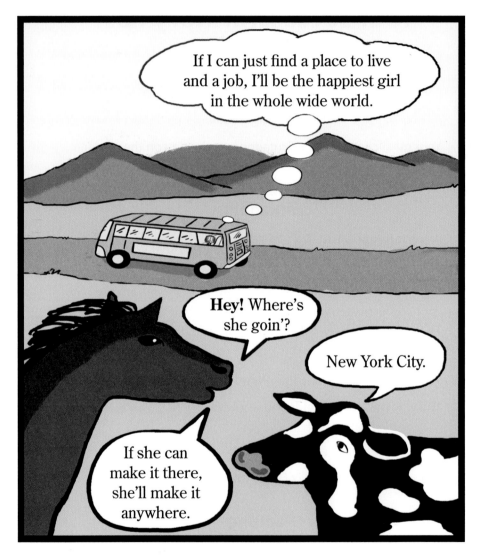

Many of the characters I write about come from small towns to a big city to fulfill their dreams. I've been there. I have felt all the mixed emotions of excitement, fear, expectation. I know that character. I know that story. I can bring it up any time and write volumes.

CHAPTER TWO

Draw, Draw, Draw

And after you finish drawing, draw some more.

Never leave home without paper and a pencil.

Sketches are quick drawings. Don't worry how they look—they're only sketches. Sketches are practice drawings just for you. The more you practice the better you get.

You never know where or when inspiration will come, so always be prepared with paper and a pencil. Have you ever had a brilliant idea one minute and then forgotten it the next? You might think that if it was genius, you would never have forgotten it. That probably is true, but why take chances? Write it down.

Sketchbooks come in all different sizes and shapes.

Are you a pocket person?

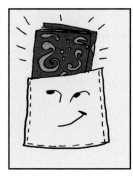

Or are you a big sketch book person?

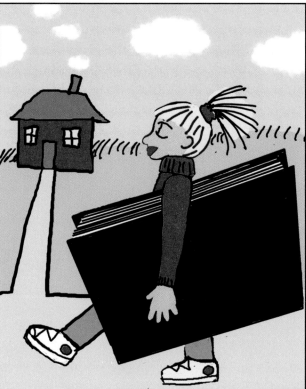

Do you like the long legal pad that you can write on for days and still have plenty of paper left over?

Or do you like to sketch in a book that has a shape?

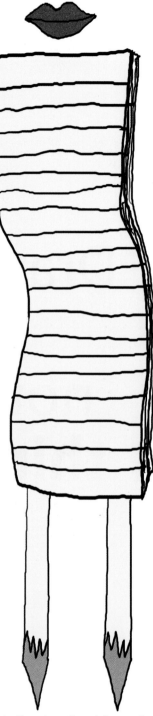

Whichever of the thousands of notebooks, legal pads, lined, unlined, bound, or unbound books you look at, find the one that is *you* and never leave home without it.

Draw what you **see**, not what you **think** you see.

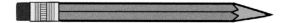

As you get older, you get used to seeing your surroundings. You might stop really *looking* at houses, trees, birds, objects in your room, or even your friends. You might draw what is in your head (what you think you see) rather than looking at what is *really* there. *Pretend you just landed from Mars and are seeing things for the first time.*

Observe a tree *as if for the first time …*

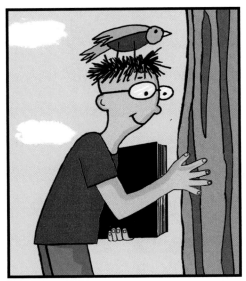

See a dog *as if for the first time …*

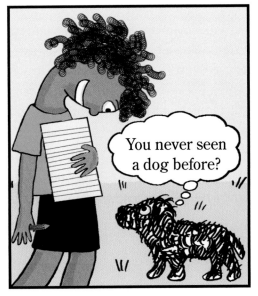

Look at yourself *as if for the first time* …

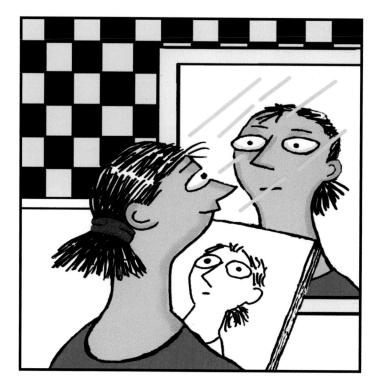

Take a good look. Do you see something new? Do you see something that you have never seen before? Is one eye lower on your face than the other? Is your right profile different than your left?

Do you remember your early drawings that you are probably embarrassed to look at now because they are so bad? Well, they may not be as bad as you think. There probably was a lot of freedom in your lines. Do you remember when you were little and scribbling with a big red crayon? Do you remember the feeling of total abandon? Did you feel free? You were probably drawing for the first time!

The art critic, Rose Slivka, said when artist Jackson Pollock tossed bright colored paint from his bucket onto canvas, it was Jackson trying to be a kid again. His paintings now sell for millions. *Have fun! You* be a kid again!

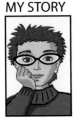

Draw from Life

In high school, I was always considered good at drawing, so it was no surprise when I got chosen to be in an advanced art class. My art teacher, Mr. Firestone, gave the class an assignment to fill up a whole sketchbook that was to be handed in at the end of the quarter.

I worked every day drawing perfectly perfect pictures. I copied them from newspapers, comic books, and magazines. All my friends and relatives oohed and ahhed at my amazing artistic ability.

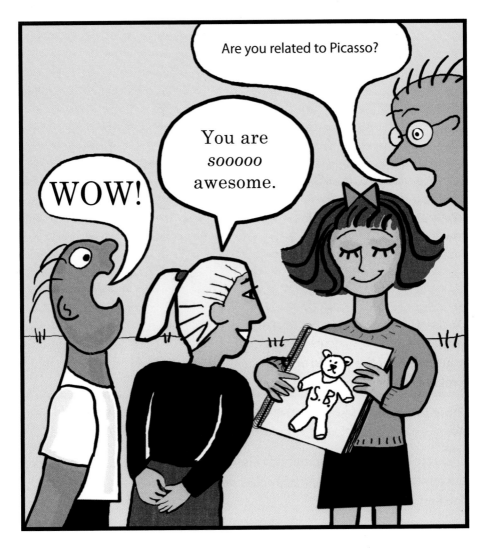

When the quarter ended, I handed in my sketchbook and was positive I would get an A+. I was *shocked* when I opened it to see a C- scribbled over one of my perfectly perfect drawings! I was sure Mr. Firestone had either lost his mind or eyesight.

Then Mr. Firestone bellowed …

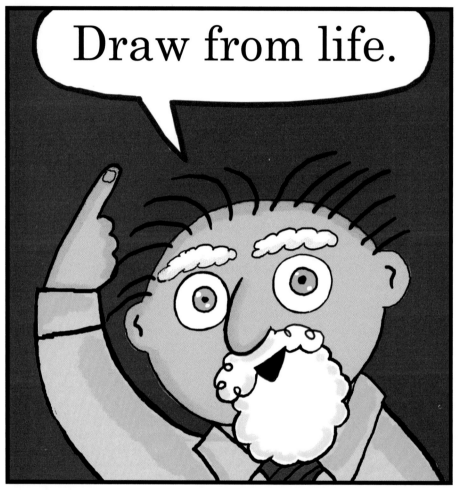

Those three words resonated. The next quarter I drew from life and got an A+.

If you are going to copy somebody else's drawings, that is okay for practice but remember, *they are somebody else's drawings.* Draw, draw, draw, until you find your own style.

CHAPTER THREE

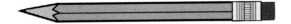

The Creative Process

is really about getting to know yourself.

20 Creative Tips

1. Ask yourself ...

Do I like being alone?

How do I react
to criticism?

Am I a morning
person or a night owl?

Do I work better with
or without music?

Where do I
work best?

Am I good under
pressure?

2. Keep a journal about your process.

A **journal** is a daily record about you. The sooner you know how you work, the better off you will be. You may learn things about yourself that even you didn't know!

3. If you don't know what you're doing, that's a good start.

Not knowing is really about allowing anything to happen.

4. Inspiration is everywhere.

Keep your eyes and ears open.

5. If you don't like being by yourself, find a partner.

If you cannot find a partner, music or talk radio may help keep you company during your time at the drawing board.

6. Make lots and lots of mistakes.

That's why erasers were invented. Try not to get frustrated. Mistakes take you to the next level.

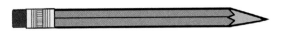

7. Art or story ... which comes first?

It doesn't matter. When doing a graphic novel or comic book there are two essential parts, art and story. Which comes first is one of those arguments that nobody wins. Many successful pages are the ones when art and story come at the same time. The creative process works differently for everybody.

If you are **character driven,** you will probably create your characters first.

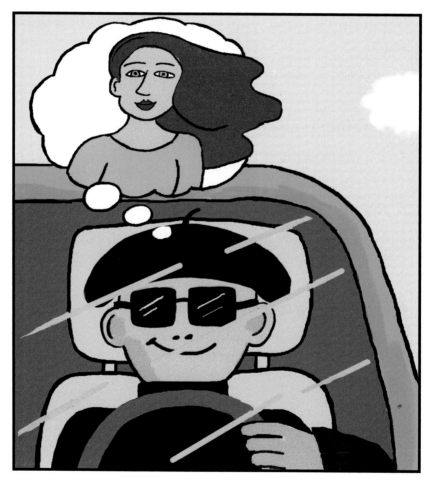

If you are **story driven,** you will probably do the story first.

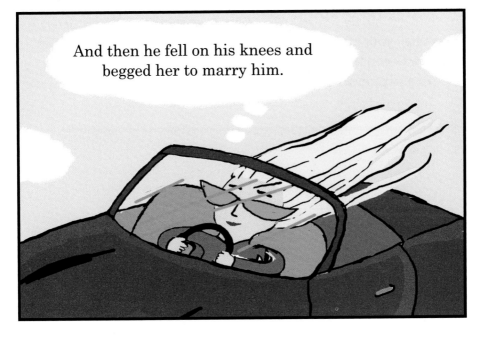

If you are just driven and go back and forth between story and art, then it doesn't matter where you begin as long as you get going.

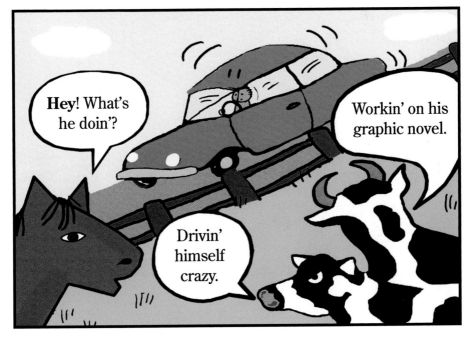

8. Don't throw anything away until you are finished with your graphic novel.

Put all your ideas, drawings, and scraps of paper into your Idea Box. Going back to your first thought may end up working on second or even third thought.

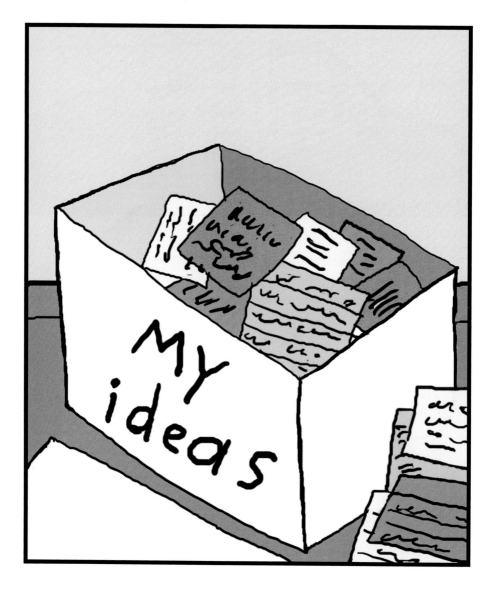

9.   It takes three.

Three men were walking down the street …

Have you ever heard a joke begin, "There were four men walking down the street?" Probably not, and that is because four is too many and becomes boring. One is not enough, two is getting there, and *three is perfect.*

It takes three words to describe your character …
Joe is seventeen, forgetful, and a loner.

Of course you will know more about Joe than just three things. However, you will get a good picture of your character in just three words.

It takes three times before it becomes a personality trait.

If Joe wakes up in the morning and cannot find his books for school, you may get a hint that he loses things. If that afternoon, Joe cannot find his pencil, you are pretty sure he is forgetful. But if later that night, Joe loses his money, you know this guy loses everything.

Three things on a list is enough.

When you are making a list, three items is the magic number. If your character is going to the supermarket, it becomes boring if you list everything that he/she bought. If you list three items—apples, orange juice, and tea—that is enough for your reader.

10. Get used to it.

Creative people have always been labeled as odd, weird, eccentric. Most people thought Vincent Van Gogh was crazy. When he was alive, the only person who bought his paintings was his brother. At auction, his last Sunflower painting sold for $40 million! The sooner you do not care what people say about you, the better off you will be.

11. Collaborate.

If you really are an artist, not a writer, then find a partner who writes. And if you really are a writer, not an artist, find a partner who draws. Some of the best graphic novels are **collaborations.** When you collaborate, you work together.

If you find somebody who you work well with, then the final product may be better than it would have been if you worked alone. Paul McCartney and John Lennon of The Beatles, were both great musicians and songwriters on their own, but together they were magical!

12. Walk away.

Some days you may not be able to do your graphic novel because you have too much to do, or there has been a family problem, or the love of your life breaks up with you. (Actually, having a broken heart is a great time to write a graphic novel!) If it's one of those days when it's just not happening, then take a break. Go for a walk and breathe in fresh air. When you come back to your drawing board, you will see your work with new eyes.

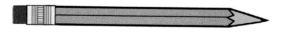

13. Recognize your breakthroughs.

A **breakthrough** is when you have struggled hard enough and long enough that you finally see things clearly. You will probably wonder why it took you so long to see something that is so obvious. *Do not give yourself a hard time. You never could have seen the light without going through your creative process.*

Before breakthrough …

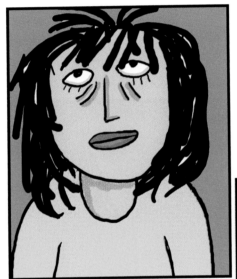

After breakthrough …

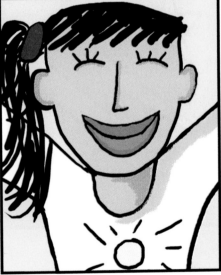

When you have a breakthrough you may want to celebrate, call a friend, or pat yourself on the back. It is good to acknowledge your great achievement. Then get back to work!

14. The Moment of Inspiration!

A famous songwriter said about one of his most successful songs, *"I wrote this song on a napkin and it only took five minutes. It wrote itself."* Obviously, the song did not write itself, but when you are truly inspired, it may *feel* that way.

Inspiration is everywhere! You might find it going for a walk, listening to music, overhearing a conversation, reading, watching TV, surfing the Internet, or observing a meteor shower. However you find inspiration, there is one thing for certain: when you get your moment of inspiration, you will know.

It might feel like a flash of lightning …

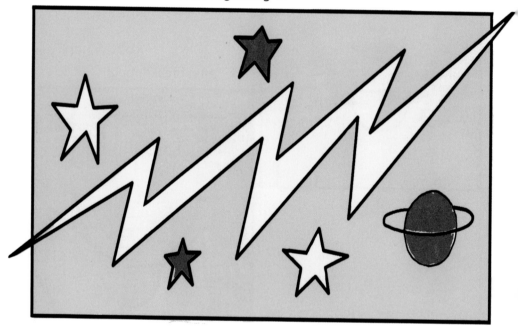

… or the heavens may open up.

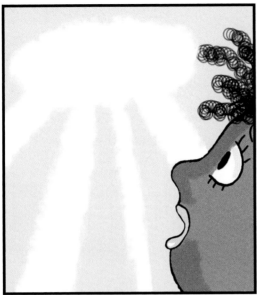

The infamous lightbulb
may go off in your head.

You may get a moment of zen …   or the big …

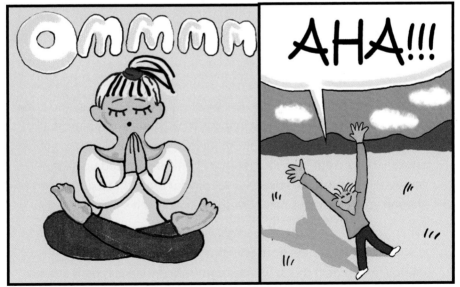

Whenever or wherever you get inspiration, be sure to write it down
in your sketchbook (that you never leave home without) before your
moment goes fleeting by.

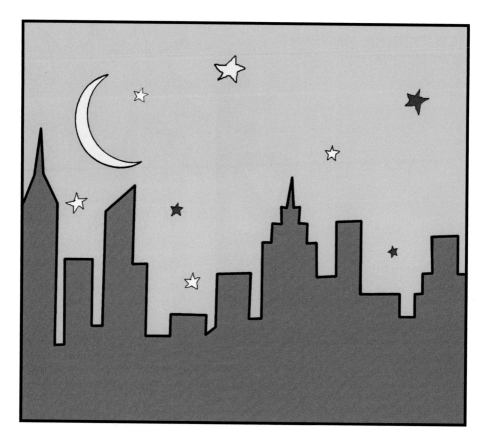

15. Go to sleep.

Have you ever worked on a puzzle before you went to sleep and knew none of the answers and then in the morning, you knew almost all of them? There is a good chance that while you were sleeping, your subconscious crept into your memory bank and looked up all the answers! (Your **subconscious** is part of your brain that exists even though your conscious mind doesn't even know it's there.)

When you sleep, it is the time to give your body and soul a rest. Sleep is when you rejuvenate from your busy day so you will have plenty of energy for the next day. It is when your subconscious is hard at work creating dreams and solving problems.

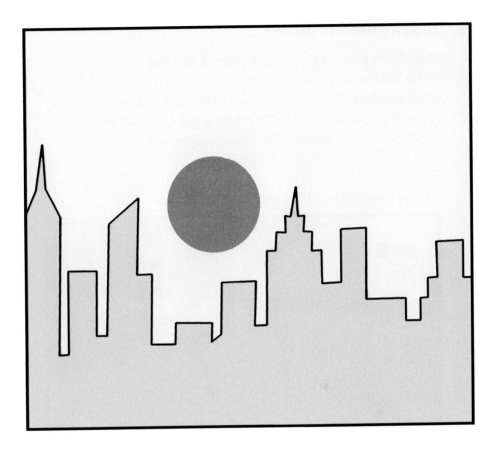

If you need an answer to a question in your story, give your subconscious an assignment. Ask yourself a question about your story before you go to sleep. Keep the question short and to the point so you will remember it. It may help you to remember if you write the question down and put it next to your bed.

As soon as you wake up, ask the same question. You may not get the answer that you will ultimately use, but something will shift and you will be able to move forward in your story.

16. Dream, dream, dream.

Dreaming is part of your creative process. You may think that you don't dream but that is not true—it's just that you aren't remembering. *Everybody dreams.* Some dreams are so obscure that they are impossible to understand while others are so clear that you may wonder if it was a dream or if it actually happened!

Always have a pencil and paper next to your bed.

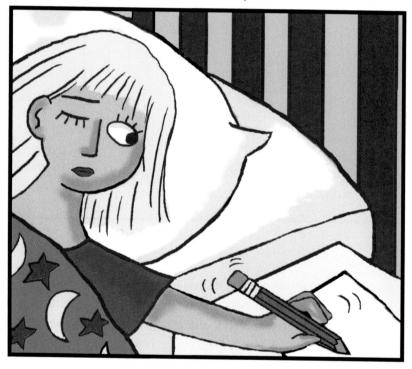

If you wake up from your dream, jot down a word or draw a quick sketch. You don't even have to turn on the light! Then go back to sleep. In the morning that jot will jog your memory and the dream will come flooding back.

Even if your dream has nothing to do with your graphic novel, have some fun and try to analyze it. Ask yourself what your dream means. The first thing that pops into your head is usually a big clue. You might get some amazing insight into yourself.

17. Switch hands.

If you feel yourself tightening up, then switch hands. Unless you are ambidextrous (using both hands equally) it will feel really weird. Your drawings will probably look like they were drawn by a 2 year old! But that's the whole idea. You need to loosen up. When you switch back to your other hand, you will feel freer.

18. You will have ups and downs.

You will have exhilarating moments and you will have frustrating ones. The exhilarating moments feel great. Those are the ones that keep you excited about your graphic novel and enable you to progress in your work. The frustrating moments are the ones where you want to throw your work into the fire. Those moments may bring anger, questions, and self-doubt. They are not easy to get through, but are just as important as the exhilarating ones.

19. Trust your process.

Don't waste time and energy second guessing yourself. You should know yourself better than anybody. If you ask too many people for an opinion, you get too many opinions. You will end up trying to please everybody and in the end please nobody.

20. Have fun!

A great thing about being creative is you get to hang with creative people. I called some of my creative friends and family and asked …

What is creativity?

enlighte

Natural way of being.

Bert Stern, Photographer and Icon

Creativity is the ability to perceive intriguing possibilities … where others only see a blank page.

Tom DeFalco, Writer & Marvel Comics Editor-in-Chief 1990-95

illumí

Making something that wasn't there before.
Richard Minsky, Artist and Founder, Center for Book Arts

genius

It has something to do with freedom.
Jane Gennaro, Actress and Voice-Over Personality

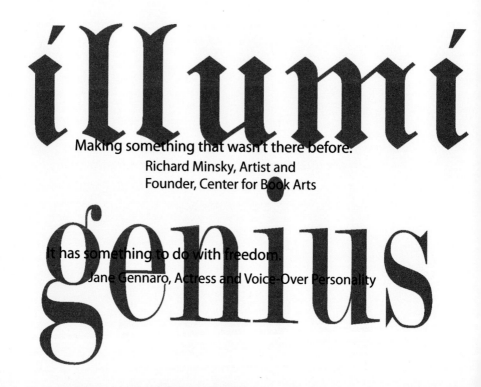

Experience a new way of looking at something and its not always pretty.
Pat Gorman, Co-Designer, MTV Logo

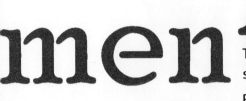

Trying to define creativity is like shoveling smoke.
Richard C. Levy, Game and Toy Inventor

VISION

Having your own vision of the world.
Paul Levitz, President and Publisher DC Comics

ration

Creativity is when the seed of a brilliant idea sprouts in your head (and heart!), grows and flowers into a bright, lovable, amusing, exciting concept, and instead of saying, "Somebody ought to do this"—you do it!

Trina Robbins, Writer/Historian, Comics Creator

MUSE

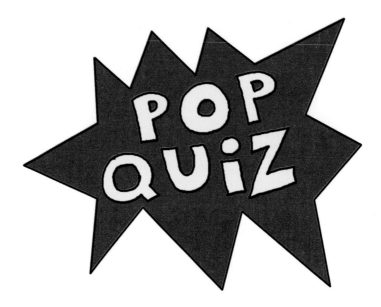

What do *you* think creativity is?

_____

_____

_____

_____

_____

Missing in Action

For several years, I worked on monthly comic books for Marvel Comics and comic strips for magazines. Although the deadlines were critical, there was always one day that my brain went M.I.A. (Missing In Action).

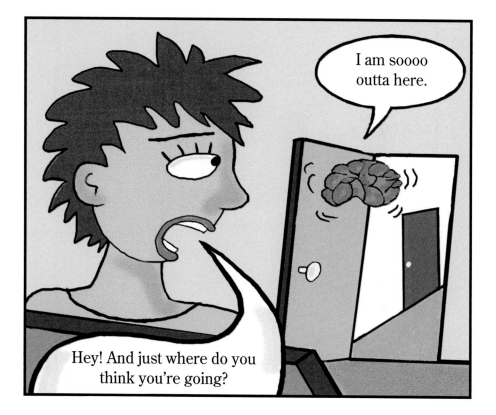

I sat at my board but couldn't write, couldn't draw. I was terrified that I would blow my deadlines (which I never did). After many hair-pulling days, the lightbulb finally went off in my head. This Missing In Action day was part of my process. (If I had kept a journal about my process like I told you to do, I probably would have figured it out a lot sooner!)

Once I caught on, I happily took the day off and did something else … roller skated, went to a movie, took a long walk, or crawled into bed and watched *Lifetime TV*. And, the next day at the drawing board was always inspirational! *Get to know your process and then trust it.*

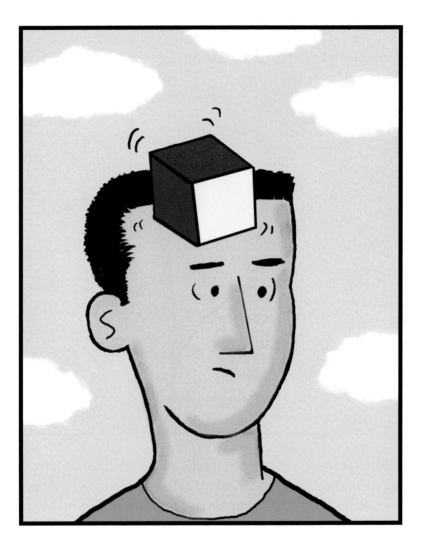

CHAPTER FOUR

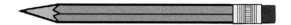

The Creative Block

Is it real?

Of course the creative block is real. But when is it *really* real and when are you using it as an excuse?

You may be using The Block as an excuse if you are just being lazy.

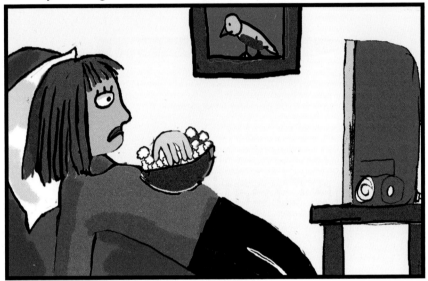

Or you are telling the world all about it.

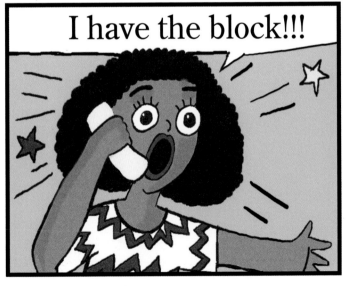

This may be your way of seeking attention. Try to get back to work. It probably is not the real thing.

You may be using The Block as an excuse if you would rather go on vacation than work.

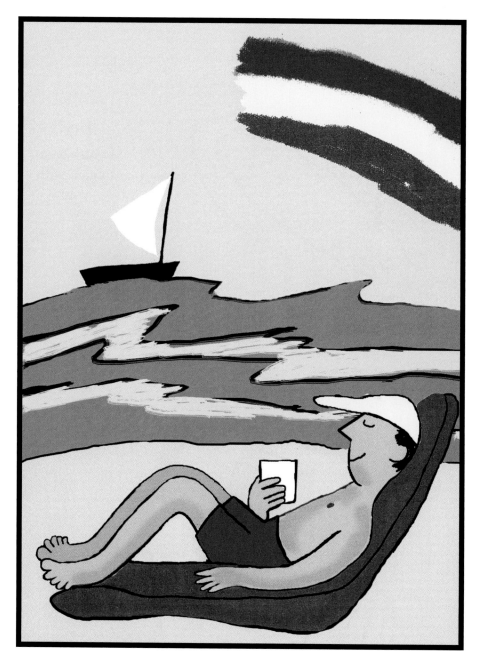

You can go on vacation and relax half the time and work on your graphic novel the other half.

Do not confuse hard work with The Block. When it's the real thing, you will know. You will think that every creative bone has left your body …

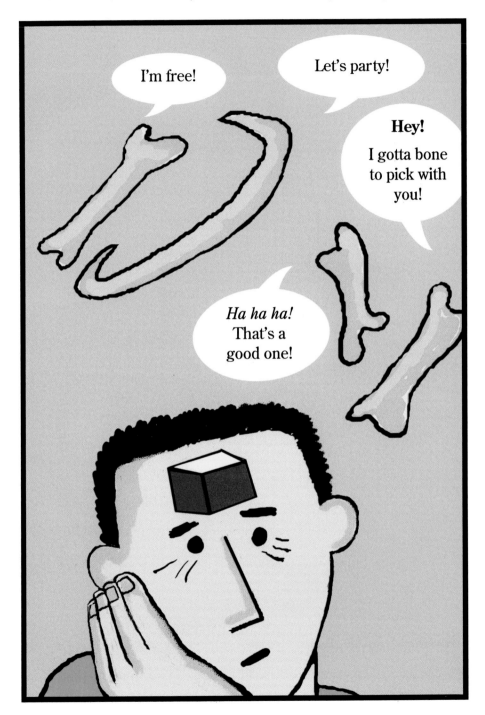

You will look at your past excellent work and wonder …

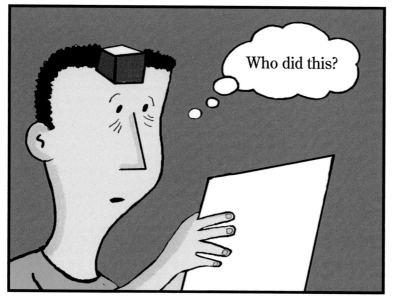

You are sure you will never be able to write or draw again.

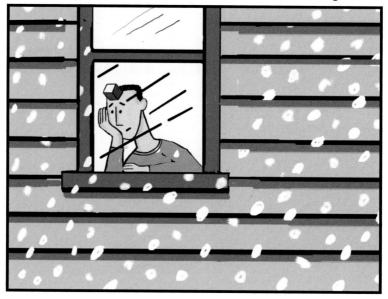

There is no easy way of dealing with The Block. Sometimes switching your focus helps. If you are blocked in your writing, then try drawing. If you are blocked in your drawing, then try writing. Figure out how *you* deal with The Block. The more you know your process, the quicker you will get unblocked.

Often the most frustrating days are the ones when you are making the most progress.

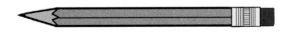

Where does The Block come from?

The creative block can come from something somebody said …

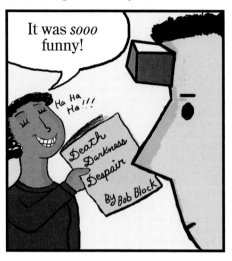

… or did not say.

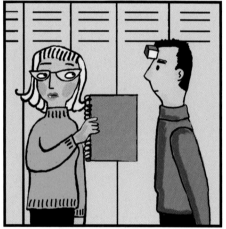

It can come from something you *thought* somebody said but they did not say it at all.

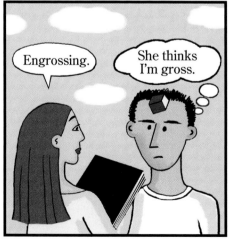

A creative block can come from anywhere.

If you have tried going over …

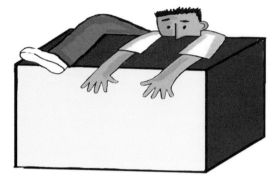

around …

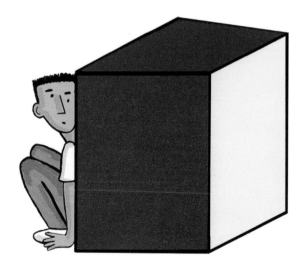

under …

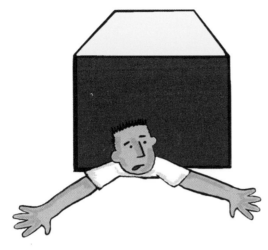

or breaking through your block …

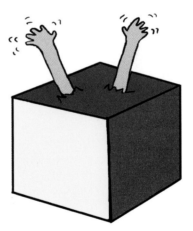

… but nothing is working, then maybe you have to go back to the point in your story where you got blocked. You may be writing about something that is difficult or painful to you. *You* might have to deal with some *issues* before you can expect your characters to deal with them.

Sometimes talking to a friend, teacher, therapist, or parent helps. Once you get to the root of your problem, you can start to deal with it and then your block will go away.

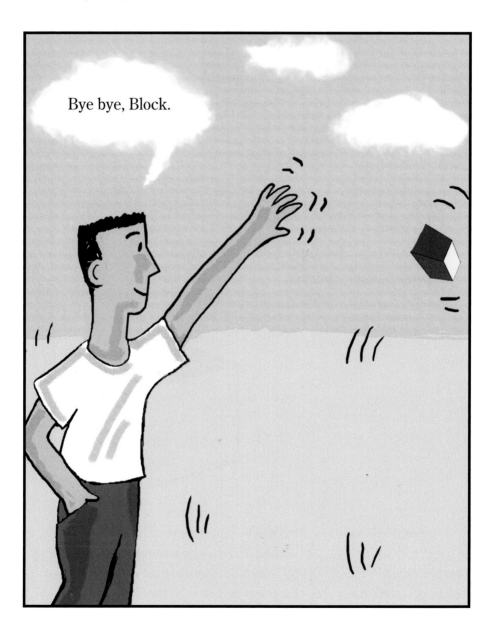

CHAPTER FIVE

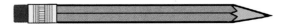

Creating Characters

They're everywhere.

Keep your eyes and ears open.

You may overhear a conversation that inspires a character or it might be a voice, an accent, or the clothes somebody wears. It could be the way somebody stands or sits or bites his lower lip. You might create a character from the way a person smells. *Characters are everywhere.*

Sometimes a character will jump right off your page …

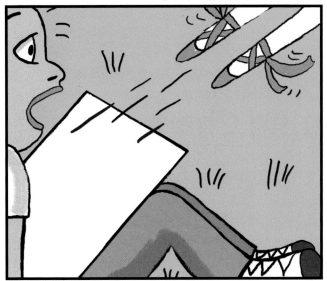

… or come to you in a dream.

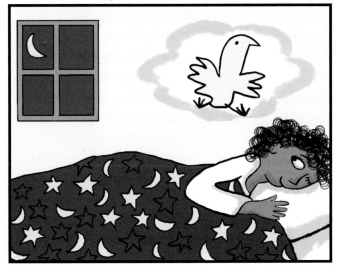

You might write about the one and only *you*.

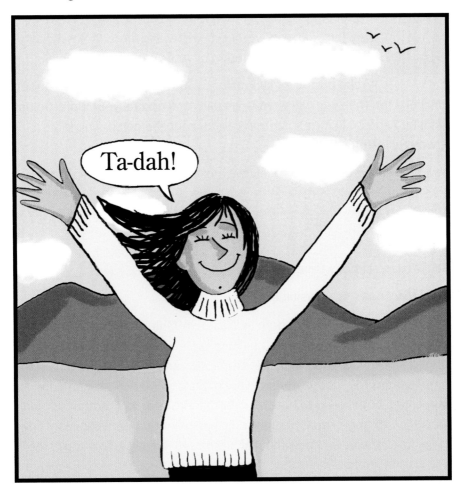

You do not have to live a fascinating life to write about a character based on *you*. Even if you think you are leading a boring life, if you write an interesting story about your boring life, then it is a good story.

Harvey Pekar wrote about his everyday life working as a file clerk in a hospital in Cleveland, Ohio. Through his graphic novel, *American Splendor,* he made his mundane existence interesting. There was even a fantastic movie based on his graphic novel.

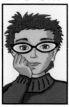

MY STORY

The "Bible"

Whether you are writing about yourself, a superhero, a fish, or your next-door neighbor, *you will need to know everything there is to know about your character and more.* Professionals call this detailed description of your character the "bible."

As you progress in your story, you will learn new things about your character. Then you will want to go back and update your bible. Do not be afraid to add or change something about your characters. This bible is not written in stone.

Below is an excerpt from the *Angel Love* bible that I created for DC Comics.

NAME: Angel Love

AGE: 18

PARENTS: Jane and Jay Love

SISTER: Mary Beth (12 years older)

CHILDHOOD: Angel Love was born in Oldstown, Ohio. Jay Love is a minister and Jane Love works as a seamstress. Angel was a happy child but all that changed when older sister Mary Beth ran away. Angel was only 6, but she remembers her mother crying every night after Mary Beth suddenly disappeared. Angel grew to hate Mary Beth for causing her mother so much pain. Although Angel remembered some harsh fighting between Mary Beth and her folks, she never knew the real reason she ran away. That topic, she knew, was off limits.

Being the daughter of a minister was not easy for Angel. She tried to set a good example in the community, she didn't like to do the things most of the other girls did like shopping or trying on lipstick. She would rather stay home and draw.

Although Angel loved her parents, she was ready to leave Oldstown the day she graduated from high school. She knew she would "fit in" better in a big city. There, she could feel free to be herself and pursue her dream of being an artist.

EDUCATION: Street smart rather than book smart. Got straight Cs except for an A in Art.

HOME LIFE: Shares an apartment on West 106th street with Wendy Thornball, a struggling actress. The furniture is collected from the streets. Angel was shocked to learn that some New Yorkers threw out practically new stuff!

EMPLOYMENT: Works four nights a week as a waitress at Balloon Restaurant. The salary from this job covers rent and expenses. During the day, Angel is either at her drawing board or looking for work as an artist.

LEISURE ACTIVITIES: Drawing cartoons, roller-skating, and collecting treasures from the garbage.

CLOTHING: Angel has her own flair for fashion. She likes color and sometimes adds a streak of blue to her bright red hair. Her trademark is that she always wears hearts.

PERSONAL CHARACTERISTICS: Stubborn (a Taurus), strong-willed, ambitious, brutally honest, and finds peace by roller-skating in Central Park.

LOVE LIFE: When Angel falls, she falls hard. But that doesn't happen often.

BEST FRIEND: Cindy Lockheart. Tall, brown hair, and very opinionated. She works with Angel at the Balloon Restaurant.

NEXT DOOR NEIGHBOR: Everett is an African American 20 year old who lives down the hall from Angel and Wendy. He is very good friends with Angel and dislikes Wendy. For extra cash, Everett plays his guitar in Central Park. His girlfriend, Lola, is unhappy about his closeness with Angel.

FAVORITE COLOR: Red

CAREER GOAL: To be an employed artist.

ROOMMATE: Wendy Thornball , a spoiled, clueless, and lovable 22 year old. Wendy and Angel are friends even though they come from two different worlds.

HALO: The cartoon character that Angel draws.

Creating Characters

❋ **Give them time to develop.**
Some characters come to you quickly while others take a long time. *Trust your process.*

❋ **Draw something unique, something that nobody has ever seen before.**
Although you will be influenced by other artists, create a character that is uniquely *you.*

❋ **Hear their voices in your head.**
You are not going crazy. Sometimes your character's voice comes even before you finish your drawing. Your creation may be telling you how it wants to look, dress, or be. *Pay attention.*

❋ **Allow for accidents.**
Accidents are really your subconscious trying to tell you to take another look.

❋ **Take breaks and take walks.**
When you return, see your creation as if for the first time.

❋ **Recognize your character.**
Get a sense of who your character is just by looking at him/her/it.

Draw your character from …

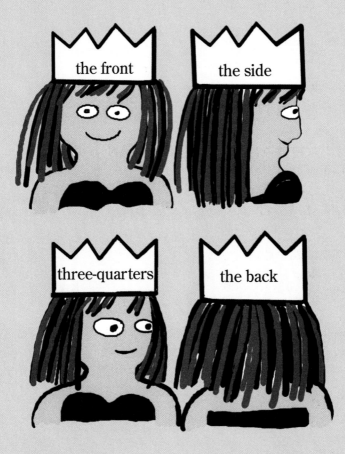

the front

the side

three-quarters

the back

Draw your character ...

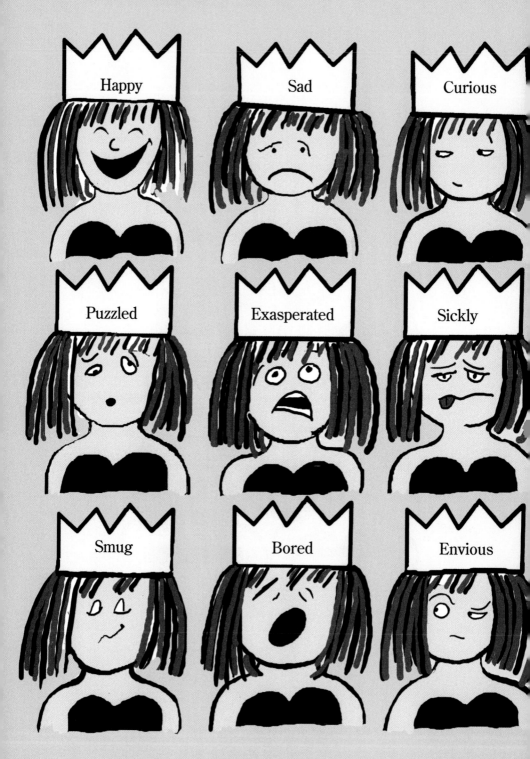

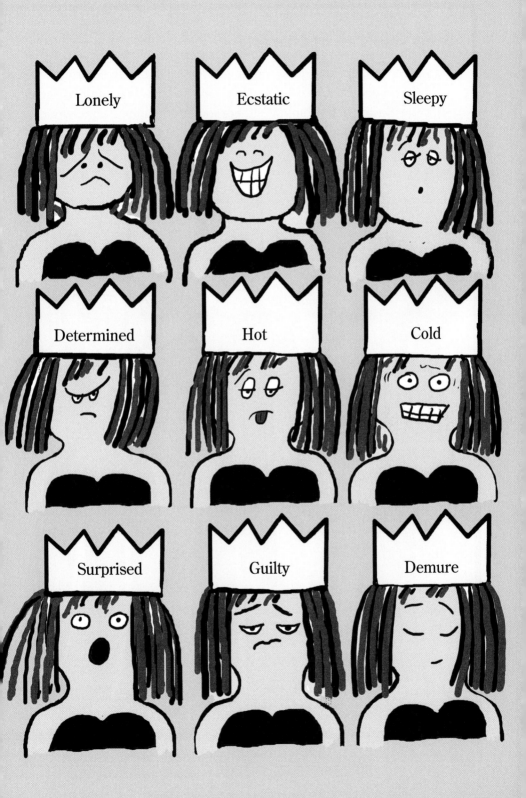

Draw your Cast of Characters

Do your characters look good together? Who is the tallest? Shortest? Roundest? Loudest? Oldest? Youngest? Do you know who your character is just by looking at her/him/it? Is there something unique about your characters? Something nobody ever saw before?

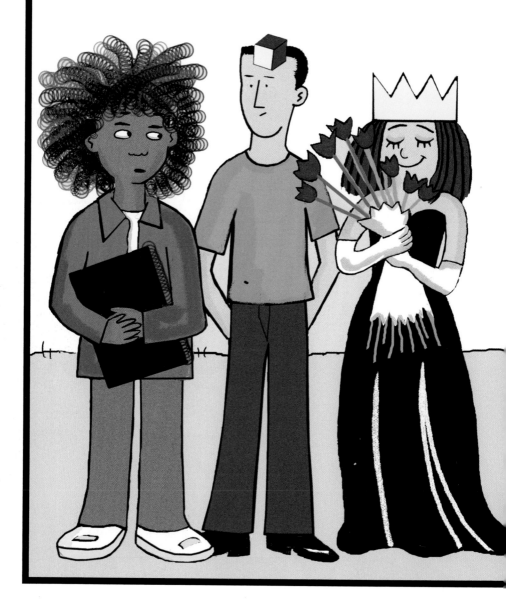

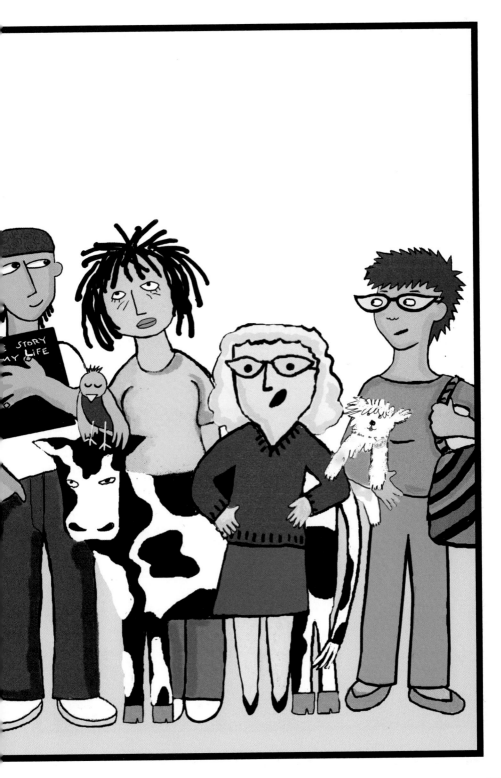

65

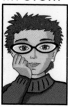

Characters are Everywhere!

I usually enjoy my visits to my local post office because the woman behind the counter is so friendly. We talk about the weather, how many more days until she retires, and then she shows me the new stamps. Together we "ooh and ahh" at the great miniature works of art.

On a recent visit, she was just about to show me the latest when the door flew open and a loud, obnoxious, cell-phoned, desperate-for-attention character charged into the post office.

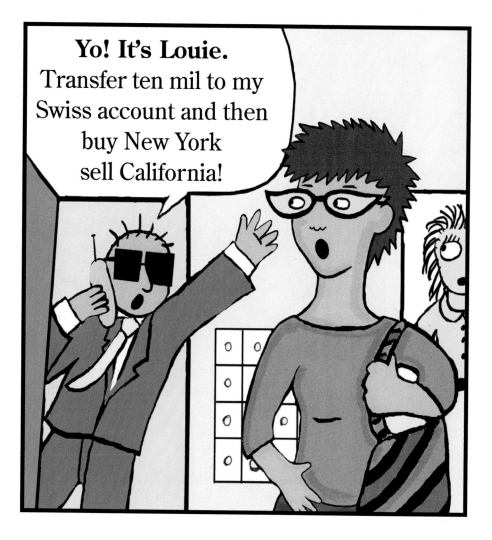

I used to say something like this …

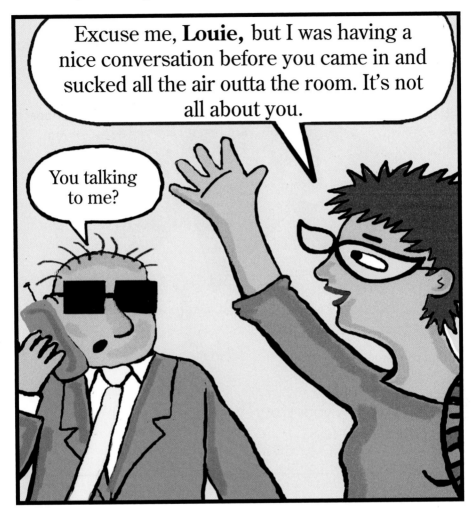

I have given up trying to reason with characters like Louie because they are unreasonable. (Maybe that is why they are called characters.) Instead, I file them away for future use. Now, whenever I need a loud, obnoxious, cell-phoned egomaniac, I go to Louie. Reliving that scene, I get the essence of Louie.

Your "go-to Louie" does not have to be a scene like the Louie one. It can be a smell, a taste, an accent, a look, or the way somebody dresses. It is the place to go when you need to conjure up your character.

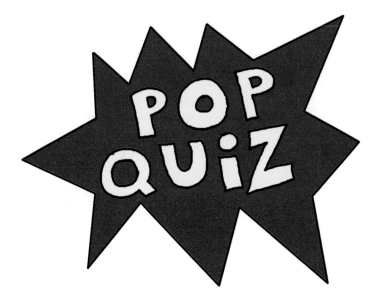

1. Do you know your story? Write it down in three sentences or less.

_____

_____

_____

_____

(Check to see if it has a beginning, middle, end, and twist.)

2. Would you be excited to read your story?

Yes 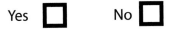 No

3. Did you write your characters' bibles?

   (Everything you need to know about your characters and more.)

Yes  No

4. Do you know your Protagonist? Antagonist? Conflict? Setting? Theme?

Yes  No

5. Is your head about to explode with ideas?

Yes  No

If you know your story, you would be excited to read it, and answered yes to 3, 4, and 5, then **CONGRATULATIONS!** *You are ready to plot.*

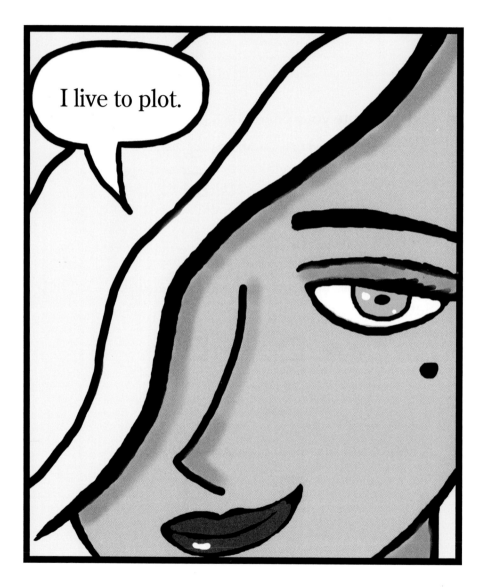

CHAPTER SIX

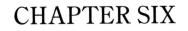

The Plotline

shows the **evolution** of your story. All its twists
and turns … highs and lows … plots and subplots.

Learning to Plot

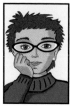

My first editor from DC Comics, Karen Berger, rejected all five of my *Angel Love* scripts. I was demoralized and thought my days as a comic book creator were over before they even began. How many more times was Karen going to shake her head sadly and send me back to the drawing board? (If I had not felt so sorry for myself, I would have felt really sorry for Karen.)

The sad truth was, the only thing I knew about plotting was back at Riverside Elementary School, plotting how to get Kenny Kase back from that horrible boyfriend-stealing Linda Lavendar.

When I first started doing comic books, the readers were 95 percent boys. (This was before the surge of Manga, the Japanese comic books. Now, just as many girls as boys are reading them.) But back then, Jenette Kahn, president of DC Comics, was looking to tap into the elusive girl market.

I had already created a successful character named Ms. Liz, a sassy, spunky feminist who appeared on greeting cards, mugs, tote bags, T-shirts, etc. She even had animated appearances on NBC's *Today Show*. Although I hadn't written a full-length story about Ms. Liz, Jenette had confidence that I could create a character for girls for DC Comics. So she summoned her two super vice-presidents, Paul Levitz and Dick Giordano, to show me step-by-step how to plot.

When I left the hour and a half meeting, my head was spinning. I had no idea if I understood one word. I took a slow walk home through Central Park and breathed in fresh air. By the time I reached my apartment, everything *click, click, clicked* into place. Immediately, I began to plot my *Angel Love* series. When I showed it to Karen, she sent me back to the drawing board, only this time to get busy writing my series. Learning to plot was one of the greatest lessons of my life.

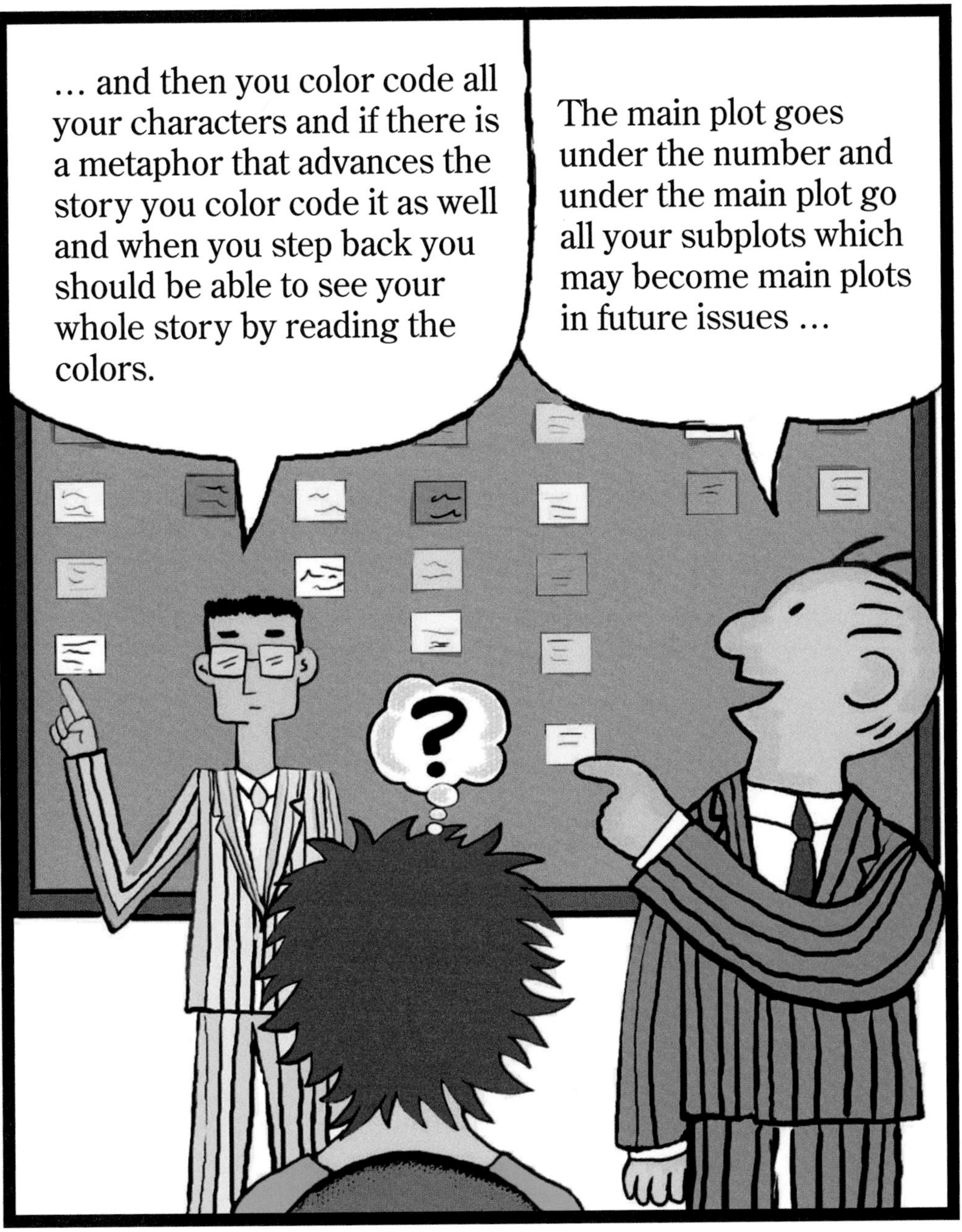
… and then you color code all your characters and if there is a metaphor that advances the story you color code it as well and when you step back you should be able to see your whole story by reading the colors.
The main plot goes under the number and under the main plot go all your subplots which may become main plots in future issues …
?

Plotting Materials

Below are the basics you will need for plotting your graphic novel. You may have available materials in your home or maybe you will want to go on a plotting shopping spree!

You can choose:

1.   A big white board (approximately 24 x 36 inches)

2.   Colored sticky notes

   (You will be constantly changing and rearranging your plotline. Sticky notes are great because they are easy to move around.)

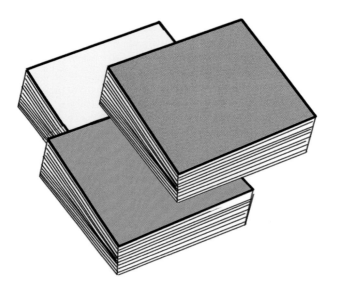

3.   A pencil

Or you can choose:

1. A bulletin board

2. Push pins

3. 5x7 note cards

4. Colored pencils or markers

Or you can plot on a computer.

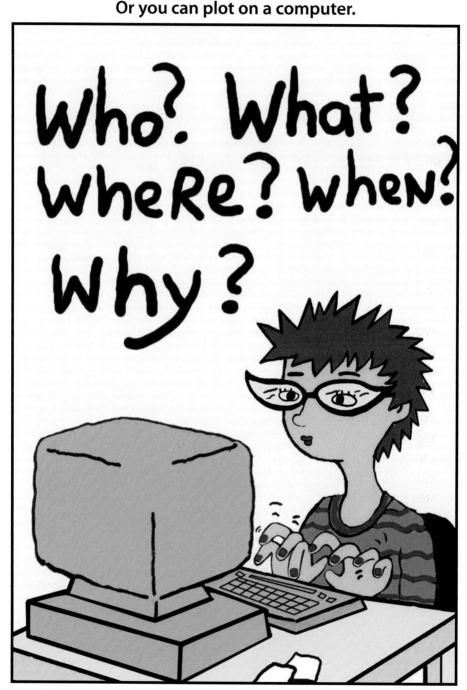

Everybody works differently. Figure out what works best for you. *Improvise!*

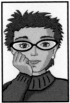

A Space of Your Own

You will be pondering, laughing, and going crazy in this space. It does not have to be a big space as long as you can claim it as your own. (If that is impossible, then be sure to find a safe spot to put your work when you are finished for the day.)

Keep dogs, cats, brothers, sisters, parents, girlfriends, boyfriends, and roommates out. Make the space *you*. If you collect action figures and like looking at them, then put them in your space. If you prefer adorable bunnies, pictures of your boyfriend, girlfriend, family, or an inspirational figure, then put that in your space.

I used to have a really bad habit of asking everybody and their mother for an opinion. After years of getting conflicting advice on everything, I realized that my first thought was almost always right. I needed to remind myself on a daily basis that *"I know best."*

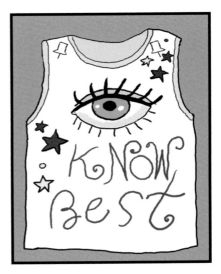

One day, my friend Pat Gorman invited my daughter, Samantha, over to her house to paint T-shirts. I decided to join in on the fun and painted my motto, "I know best," on a T-shirt. It is hanging on the wall above my computer and I look at it every day.

Do you have a creed, motto, or mantra that is *you?* Do you remind yourself of your motto to make yourself feel better or to help you make a decision? Or is your motto more about how you view life? What is *your* motto? Put it in your space.

How to Plot

Before you begin, see my *Angel Love* plotline on pages 100 and 101. It probably won't make much sense at first, but it will give you an overview of what a plotline looks like.

1. Write your story line on an index card. It has a beginning, middle, end, and twist.

(Remember! It can take many pages to write and draw your graphic novel but you should be able to tell your story in three sentences.)

> The Adventures of Normal Boy
> My story is about a boy who is strong enough to lift the Empire State bldg., fast enough to fly around the world in 5 seconds flat and agile enough to morph into any form he chooses. The only thing he can't do but wants more than anything is to Be Normal.

Keep your index card next to your plotline. Being able to quickly refer to what your story is about will keep you on track when you plot. You may decide that what you thought was your story is not it at all. If you decide to change it, then write that story on an index card.

2. Give your story a "working title."

A **working title** is one that works for the time being. Write it on top of your index card. Your title may change many times but while you are working on your graphic novel, it is important to have a name for it. Many writers do not know the real name of their story until their graphic novel is all finished.

3. Number the top of your board.

(Using a board is just one way of plotting. Improvise! For my *Angel Love* series, I taped together 8½ × 11 paper and used colored pencils.)

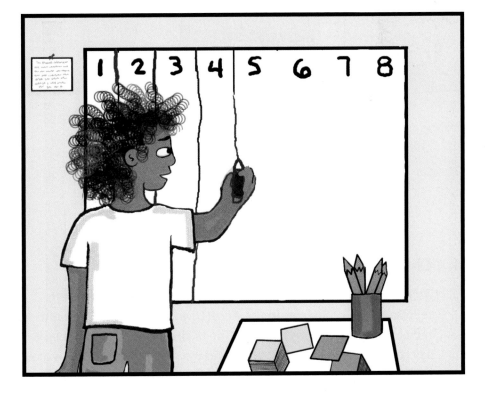

The numbers represent the chapters of your graphic novel. You probably will not know the exact number so make a rough guess. If you are doing a comic series then these numbers represent your monthly books. (Many serialized comic books have been turned into graphic novels.)

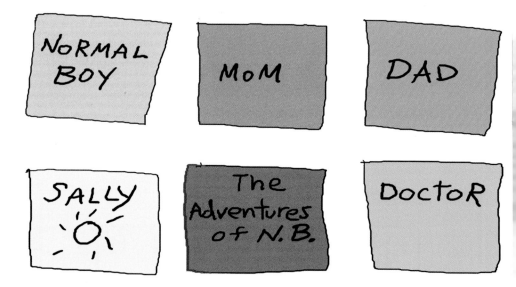

4. Choose your colors.

Assign each character a color. Choose a color that you think best represents your character. In the *Angel Love* series, Angel has bright red hair so I chose red as her color. The talking cockroaches are black so I chose black to represent them, and the neighborhood bum is gray to represent his sad life out on the streets of New York City. There may be other things you will want to color code that are recurring themes in your story such as a dream, a city, or a sunset.

In *The Adventures of Normal Boy,* the creator chose the colors above. Sally, Normal Boy's girlfriend, is yellow, representing sunshine. Normal Boy feels sunny and bright when he is with her! He chose orange for Normal Boy's big adventures.

5. Write your scene.

Think about what is happening in the scene. Write it down in as few words as possible.

> At age 5 NORMAL BOY (N.B.) realizes he can fly but nobody else can. He begins to keep his power to fly a secret.

This quick note is to jog your memory. (You will be able to write the entire scene later.) But for now, you are plotting your story. If you want to draw a quick sketch to tell you what the scene is about, then do that. As long as you understand what is happening in each scene, that is all that matters. Don't worry how it looks.

Be sure to color code. Decide who is the lead character. Then choose his/her/its color. Normal Boy is assigned the color blue, so every time he is the main character in your scene, then you will choose a blue sticky note (or blue pencil, marker, or a blue from your color palette if you are using a computer).

Plotting is when all those brilliant ideas that have been twirling and swirling around in your head can come out and take form.

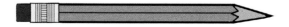

6. Write as many scenes as you know or think you know.

Look in your Idea Box. Get out your sketchbooks, scraps of paper, your journal, or anything else where you wrote ideas about your graphic novel.

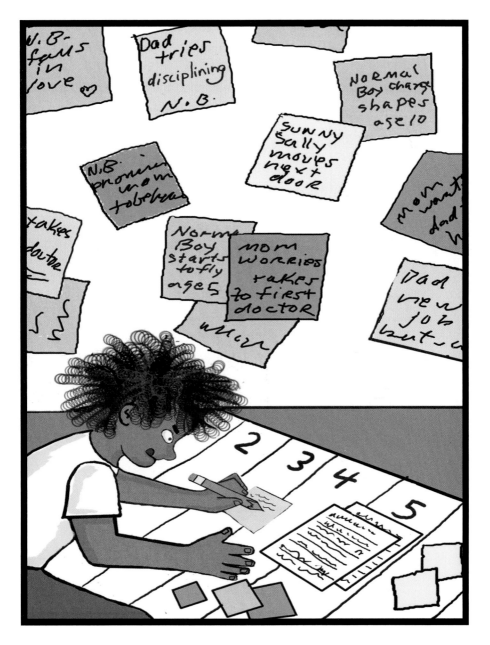

7. Main plot and subplots.

N.B. is BORN
MoM and
Dad discover
Something is
WRONg.

MoM catches
N.B. Reading
at 6
MoNthS

Dad sees N.B.
Can fix
his BRoKeN
CAR
ENGine.

MoM + Dad don't
want to scare
each other, so
they both
take N.B. to
DR. SECRetly.

The **main plot** goes on the top, directly under your chapter number. **Subplots** go underneath the main plot. Subplots are just what they sound like. They are not the main plot, they are secondary ones. A subplot can start out that way, and become a main plot in a future chapter or series. In the *Angel Love* plotline, the Everett storyline (blue) is introduced in the first issue as a subplot, and evolves into the main plot in the third issue.

If you are doing a comic book series, a reader may pick up your series in the third, fourth, or ninety-ninth issue. Every issue must be able to grab the reader's attention with a compelling story. It is important to have a main plot in every issue. That is, one with a beginning, middle, end, and twist. If you have too many subplots, and not a strong main plot, then there's a good chance that you might lose a reader.

8. Organize your story.

Every scene advances your story. All your plots and subplots will have their own story with twists and turns. Be sure they are in the right order. Some plots and subplots will intersect with each other. That is, your storylines will come together in a scene. It may be difficult to choose a main character because there could be two or even three main ones. You may want to use more than one sticky note to color code that scene. However, if possible, try to choose one main character to color code. It will be easier to read in the end.

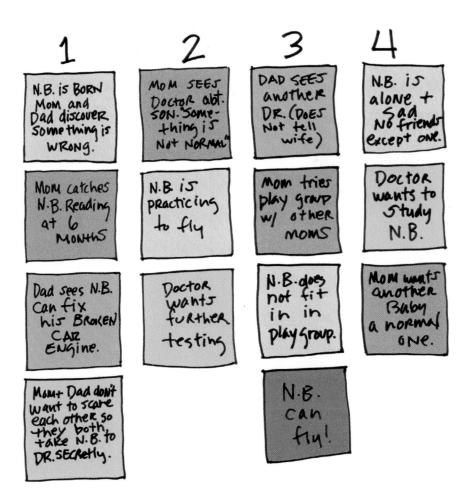

1

N.B. is BORN
Mom and
Dad discover
Something is
WRONG.

Mom catches
N.B. Reading
at 6
MONTHS

Dad sees N.B.
Can fix
his BROKEN
CAR
ENGINE.

Mom + Dad don't
want to scare
each other so
they both
take N.B. to
DR. SECRETLY.

2

MOM SEES
Doctor abt.
SON. "Some-
thing is
Not NORMAL"

N.B is
practicing
to fly

Doctor
wants
further
testing

3

DAD SEES
another
DR. (Does
Not tell
wife)

Mom tries
play group
w/ other
moms

N.B. does
not fit
in in
play group.

N.B.
can
fly!

4

N.B. is
alone +
sad
No friends
except one.

Doctor
wants to
Study
N.B.

MOM wants
another
Baby
a normal
one.

9. Step back from your plotline.

By following your color code, you should be able to see the progression of your story … all its twists and turns … highs and lows … plots and subplots.

Changing and rearranging your plotline is part of your plotting process. However, if you are going to make a major transformation, make a copy of your plotline. In the end, you may decide that you like it better the way it was in the first place!

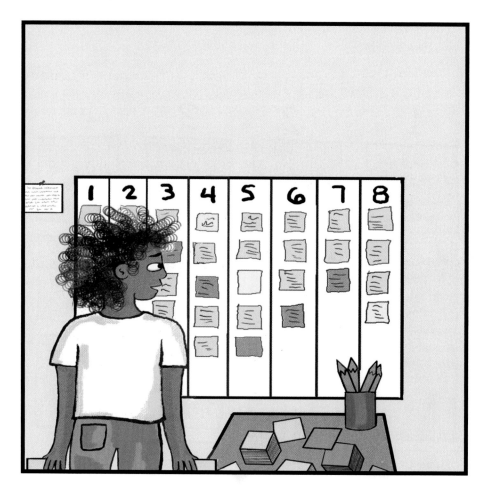

Read this chapter again and again. Plotting is not easy, but once you get it, you'll be glad you took the time to learn!

Plotting Pointers

Keep the twists and turns coming.

Nobody likes a boring story!

Keep introducing and reintroducing your characters.

Show them at work, where they live, where they hang out. The more information you can give about your characters, the better it is for your reader.

You can give a lot of information through the backgrounds in your panel. If your character is in her bedroom with a pile of dirty laundry and everything strewn all over her room, then your reader will get the picture that she is not a very neat person.

Do not push an idea into your story if it does not fit.

If an idea does not work, then no matter how funny, dramatic, or brilliant the idea is, do not include it in your graphic novel. It may destroy the continuity of your story. Put it in your Idea Box and you could use it for another story.

Ask yourself what you need in each scene to advance your story.

Sometimes your character will tell you. Write down what he/she/it has to say.

Make your bible and plotline consistent.

As you progress in your plotline, your characters should behave in ways that are compatible with their personalities. If they don't, then either change your bible or change your plotline.

Be patient.

It is easy to get frustrated. Plotting takes time, patience, creativity, endurance, and passion.

Go to sleep!

You could stay at your bulletin board all night trying to figure out your character's next move and still not have the answer. In fact, you may set yourself back.

Sometimes, all you need is a good night's sleep. In the morning, you will feel refreshed and will be able to look at your plotline with a new point of view.

Get feedback.

Talking about your plotline with a friend or advisor can help. Be sure to talk to somebody you trust and respect. Showing your story to the wrong person can be destructive and may even bring on a creative block.

Do not go on a wild goose chase.

Sometimes a character will take you in another direction from your plotline. Maybe your story needs improvement. You might go along with your character and see where he/she/it takes you.

On the other hand, if your character is taking you on a wild goose chase, you can waste hours, days, and even months of precious time. It is up to *you* to decide whether you should reign your character in or go along for the ride.

Trust your process.

If it feels right, then go there. If after you go there, it doesn't feel right, then go back to where you started.

You still have advanced in your story because you were able to see that the direction you thought would work does not and you can head off in a new direction.

Put your thoughts in your Idea Box.

Remember! Don't throw anything away until you are finished writing and drawing your graphic novel.

Sometimes an idea won't work in one place in your plotline, but fits perfectly in another place. Or there may be a drawing that you thought was a reject, but when you take another look, it turns out to inspire a whole new direction. And finally, you may decide to do a second edition of your graphic novel, and your Idea Box is just what you need to get started!

Have a few secrets.

Know things that your reader does not. In the *Angel Love* series, Mary Beth, Angel's sister, was a politician running for mayor. Even though Mary Beth was not introduced to the reader until the fifth issue, there were flyers about Mary Beth's campaign in the background in the first issue.

It's fun to have secrets and leak little hints as you plot along. Die-hard fans pick this stuff up and love it!

Have fun!

Sample Plotline

Below is a plotline based on the first six issues of the *Angel Love* series that I created for DC Comics.

1.	2.	3.
Angel falls in love with Don but finds out he's got big problems.	Angel tries to help Don with his big problem but he denies he has a problem. She breaks up with him.	Lola gives Everett an ultimatum..."Marry me OR ELSE!" Everett asks for Angel's help.
Angel works as a roller skating waitress at Balloon restaurant.	Wendy takes care of a wounded bird (Rose) that she saved in Central Park.	Wendy is obsessed with Rose and Everett sets the bird free.
Cindy works with Angel and is her best friend.	Everett writes music and plays his guitar in the park.	Halo is the cartoon angel that Angel draws
Wendy is Angel's roommate. She is rich and spoiled and thinks she's an actress/model. She practices for "Snowy Show detergent" commercial.	Lola is Everett's girlfriend who writes music with Everett and is jealous of his relationship with Angel.	Angel picks up a flyer to vote for Maureen McMeal.
Talking cockroaches live in the apartment	Cockroaches think Don is cute.	
Everett is Angel's good friend and lives down the hall.		

This method of color coding is used in screenplays, soap operas, and TV series as well as comic books and graphic novels.

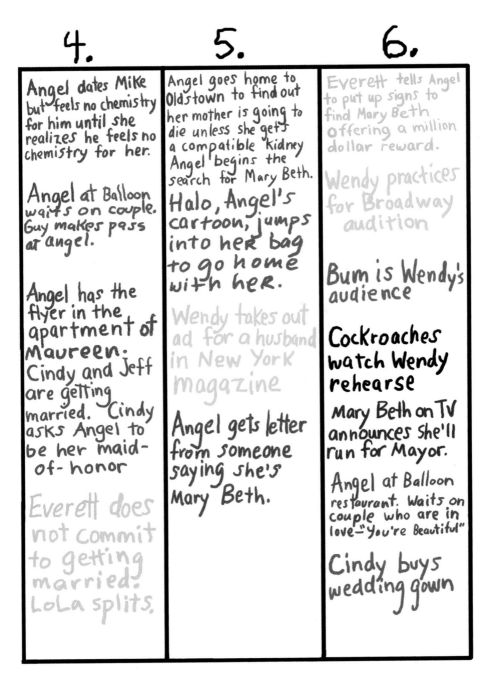

4.	5.	6.
Angel dates Mike but feels no chemistry for him until she realizes he feels no chemistry for her. Angel at Balloon waits on couple. Guy makes pass at angel. Angel has the flyer in the apartment of Maureen. Cindy and Jeff are getting married. Cindy asks Angel to be her maid-of-honor Everett does not commit to getting married. LoLa splits.	Angel goes home to Oldstown to find out her mother is going to die unless she gets a compatible kidney Angel begins the search for Mary Beth. Halo, Angel's cartoon, jumps into her bag to go home with her. Wendy takes out ad for a husband in New York magazine Angel gets letter from someone saying she's Mary Beth.	Everett tells Angel to put up signs to find Mary Beth offering a million dollar reward. Wendy practices for Broadway audition Bum is Wendy's audience Cockroaches watch Wendy rehearse Mary Beth on TV announces she'll run for Mayor. Angel at Balloon restaurant. Waits on couple who are in love—"You're Beautiful" Cindy buys wedding gown

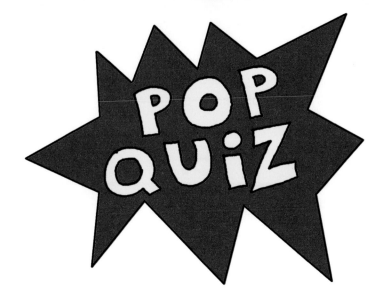

Are you ready to plot?

1. What is a working title?

2. What is a main plot?

3. If you are writing a comedy and you have a really hilarious joke, squeeze it into your story no matter what.

    True    False ☐

4. What is a subplot?

If you don't know the answers to these questions, reread this chapter.

CHAPTER SEVEN

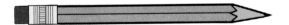

Writing

is rewriting. It is a rare writer who gets it on the first try.

You have done your homework. You have created your bible. You know your characters as well as or better than you know yourself. You have created your plotline (subject to change). Now you are ready for your characters to say everything they have to say.

If you like to work at your computer, then type away.

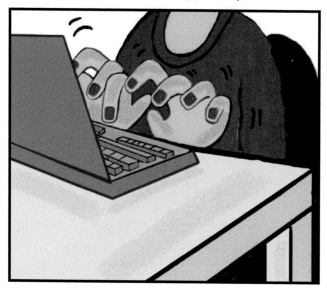

If you prefer writing in long hand, then write away.

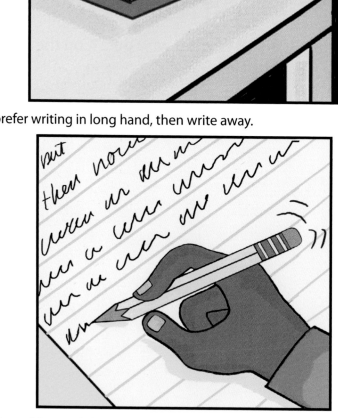

If you like writing and drawing at the same time like I do then write and draw away! *Figure out what works best for you.*

Dialogue is conversation between your characters as told to you.

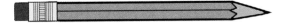

Listen to your characters. Hear their voices.

Get down as much dialogue as possible. Don't worry if your pages are messy, words misspelled, and conversation choppy. *This is just for you.* As long as you can read it, that is all that matters. You will have plenty of time to go back and make it neat when you do your rewrites.

When your characters are talking, *get out of the way.* Sometimes they are so anxious to speak that you can't shut them up. That is the time to let them speak *through* you. You chose them. Show respect. Put all thoughts, judgments, and preconceived notions aside. You are the muse. *Do not think.*

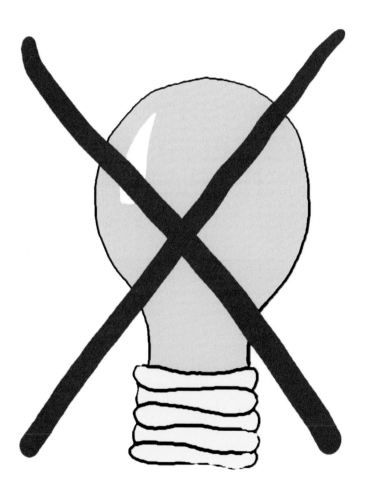

Just because you're not thinking, doesn't mean you're not the boss.

Those Voices in My Head

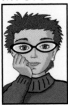

Sometimes you get to write characters that come from somebody else's head. In the 1990's Marvel Comics licensed the rights from The Walt Disney Company to publish their characters. Hildy Mesnik, my marvelous Marvel editor, invited me to write Disney's *Beauty and the Beast* comic, a spin-off of the hugely successful 1991 Academy award-winning film. She thought I was perfect for the romantic love story between Belle and the Beast. Disney commissioned only four books, because after all, they wondered, "How many stories can you write about a girl being stuck in a castle with a Beast?"

On Hildy's desk sat a box filled with the *Beauty and the Beast* movie video, a copy of the movie script, character studies, drawings, and the bible. The box weighed twenty pounds. *Literally.* I picked it up, hailed a taxi, and immersed myself in the *tale as old as time.* Belle, the Beast, Mrs. Potts, Chip, Cogsworth, and Lumiere all danced around in my head. I studied all the materials, was awestruck by the drawings, read and reread the script, and watched the movie over and over. Suddenly, Cogsworth and Lumiere started bickering!

Once the voices were inside my head, I was good to go.

The characters fought for their spots in the comic. They were so loud and insistent that sometimes I couldn't sleep. Lumiere swore it was Cogsworth's fault, and Cogsworth insisted it was just the opposite. The stories spilled out.

Oh, and how many stories can you write about a girl being stuck in a castle with a beast? Instead of just four, we ended up doing thirteen issues.

The Narrative Voice

The narrative voice is the one that tells the story. It could be *your* voice or one of your characters' voices. The narrative voice usually appears on the top of the panel. Some graphic novelists include the voice inside the panel and it pops up whenever the writer chooses. It is up to you to decide if you want or need a narrative voice and where and when it fits into your story.

Often the splash page includes a narrative voice. It sets the time, place, and mood. Below is a splash page, using the narrative voice.

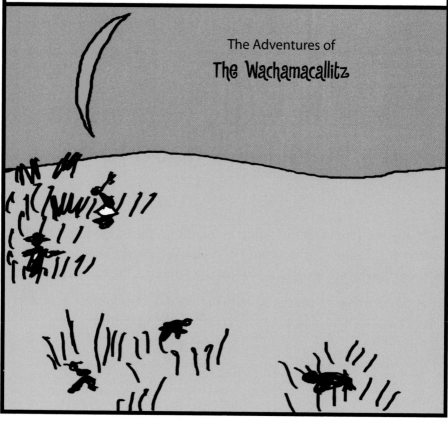

Often the narrative voice is used to transition from one scene to another by using popular phrases like these:

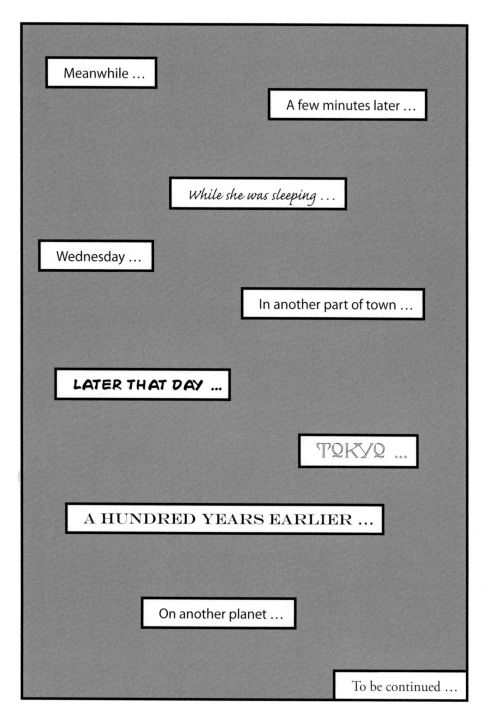

Writing Tips

Just do it.

Some writers like to start at the beginning of their story and work their way through, while others start with the most inspirational scenes. Do you have a scene in your plotline that you are just dying to write? Are your characters screaming to be heard? If the inspiration is there, then *just do it*. If your plotline is strong and your characters evolved, then it doesn't matter if you start at the beginning, middle, or end as long as you get going.

Take a scene from your plotline.

Decide what needs to be accomplished in the scene. Ask what your character needs to achieve his/her/its goal. To what length will your character go to achieve it?

Ask how your characters are feeling.

Are they happy, sad, pensive, depressed, angry? There can be more than one feeling going on.

Have you ever felt happy and sad at the same time?

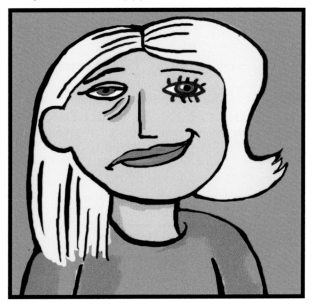

Every panel advances the story.

Keep your process moving forward. Try not to get bogged down by details, especially in the beginning of your writing. Keep the big picture in mind.

Read your dialogue out loud.

Sometimes when you read out loud, you can hear if your dialogue rings true to your character. You will also hear if it is too wordy or maybe not wordy enough.

Get in and out of the panel quickly.

Write what is needed and then go to the next panel. If you discover that you need more dialogue in your panel, you can always add it when you're doing your rewrites.

Pace your pacing.

Pacing is the way your story moves. Your story may go from fast paced to slow paced to somewhere in the middle all in the same story. Everyone goes at their own speed.

Sometimes the panels in a slow paced graphic novel are so beautifully drawn that you will need the slowness to take in the awesome art. Other times, fast paced panels are necessary when your story needs to move really quickly. In most super hero comic books, there is a fight scene that can go on for as many as 8 pages with lots of sound effects **(BLAM! WHACK! KA-POW!)**. These pages read *faster than a flying bullet.* Pacing depends on the action, mood, and drama of your story.

Feel the rhythm.

When I finish a chapter, I like to put the layouts on my bulletin board and then step back and observe them. When the pacing is perfect, the story has a rhythm to it. When you read it, you don't stop until you are finished. If along the way something stops you, then there is something wrong with the story. Many times it is the pacing. You may have too many dialogue balloons or too few. Try taking out or adding a balloon.

Turn off your critical voice.

There may be times when a voice in your head stops you from hearing your characters. You might have several voices but there usually is one main voice that will not go away. It is called your critical voice.

If your characters are *not* talking, then try to relax and *clear your head*. Close your eyes and go somewhere in your mind where you feel safe, secure, and relaxed. It could be lying on the beach listening to the waves crashing against the shore, or it could be sitting in your grandmother's kitchen.

The sooner you can clear your brain, the quicker your characters will begin to speak. Try to get your critical voice to go away.

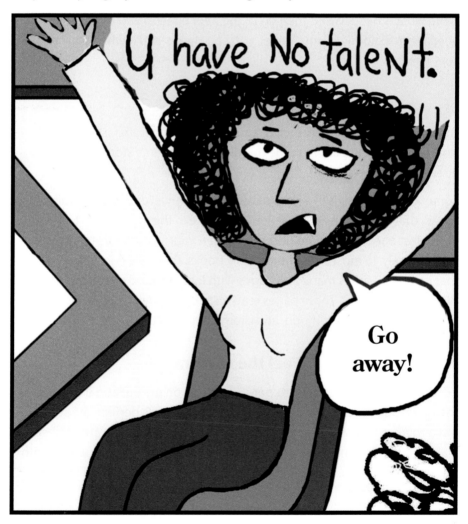

If the voice won't go away, then try to reason with it.

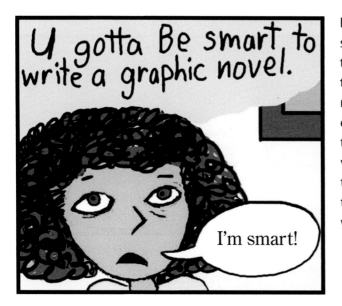

If the critical voice still won't go away, then let it rip. Give the voice a good minute to say everything it wants to say. The critical voice will tell you things about yourself that are not true. It will cause self-doubt.

Try to figure out whose voice it is. It may be a parent, a sibling, a teacher, your best or worst friend. It could be that the critical voice is not even aware that it is being critical! If the voice sounds really familiar, don't be alarmed. It just might be yours!

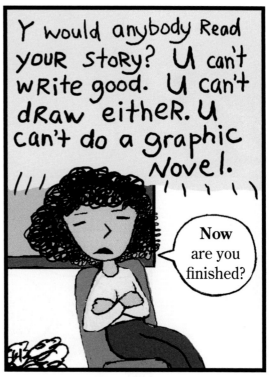

Hopefully yes! Eventually, even your critical voice will get bored and will drift away. Then get back to work. *Beware!* The voice will probably return.

Go with the flow.

Sometimes the dialogue comes easily …

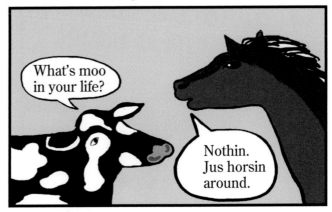

… other times a character has nothing to say.

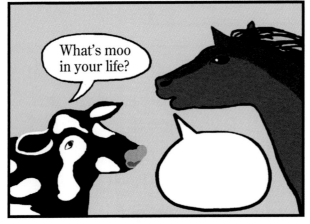

If you are stuck, leave the balloon blank and go to your next panel. Don't stop the dialogue flow.

Your character may have several answers.

It is up to you to choose. The answer may be all three!

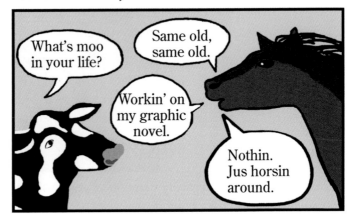

Write.

Expressing your ideas through Twittering, your blog, diary, journal, e-mail, letters, text messaging, or your graphic novel are good ways to always keep a hand in writing. *Write every day.*

Read.

Probably everyone from your first grade teacher to your parents told you to read, read, read. Well, here comes another one! You are probably already reading every graphic novel you can get your hands on. Reading other types of books may also inspire you. Many graphic novelists get their inspiration from science, fantasy, or history books. What books have inspired you?

Have the art advance your story.

The difference between an illustrated book and a graphic novel is that the art in the illustrated book illustrates the story. In a graphic novel the art advances the story. If you draw your character's room piled with dirty laundry, cats eating from bowls, and last weeks' pizza strewn on the floor, then your reader will assume that your character is a slob. You don't have to write, "Joe is a slob."

Write a script.

A script is the written form for dialogue. Some scripts are very detailed with a lot of description and direction, and others have very little. If you are the writer *and* the artist, then your script will probably have less description and direction. You can draw quick sketches or write quick notes to yourself.

If you are collaborating and you are the writer, then your script will probably be more detailed than if you were doing the art and story. *Do not feel the need to describe every minute detail.* It will stop the flow of dialogue. Besides, it is up to your artist to visualize the page the way he/she sees it.

It takes time and effort for a writer and artist to be on the same page. (Pardon the pun.) The more you work with an artist, the more you will understand what you need to put into your script and what you can leave out.

Read a script.

Page 22 THE ADVENTURES OF NORMAL BOY

Panel One: Typical doctor's office. Mom sits opposite doctor. On a table are medical magazines. Worried Mom is holding 6 month Jason (Normal Boy) in her arms.

Mom: There's something wrong, doctor. He's not normal!

Doctor looks at bored Jason.

Doctor Epstein: *(smiles condescingly)* He looks normal to me, Mrs. Scott.

Panel Two: Closeup of wise Doc.

Doctor Epstein: Sometimes first time mothers tend to worry a little too much. It's only natural.

Panel Three: long shot with Mom, Jason and Doctor.

Mom: But Doctor Epstein, he's only 6 months old and he's reading already!

Doctor Epstein *(throwing head back in hilarious laughter)*: Ha, ha, ha.

Panel Four: Bored Jason reaches for magazine.

Dr. Epstein: Oh Mrs. Scott! Every mother thinks their child is a genius. Don't push him. By the time he's in first grade, he will learn to read.

Panel Five: Jason opens the magazine. Doc continues lecture.

Doctor Epstein: In the meantime, Mrs. Scott, I want you to get out more and try to meet with frien-

Jason *(interrupting)*: The best way to stay fit is to eat plenty of vegetables and fruits and make sure you exercise at least 30 minutes a day.

Panel Six: Doctor does double take!

Panel Seven: Doctor jumps up on chair.

Doctor Epstein (shouting): Mrs. Scott, your boy is not normal!

Mom *(frustrated)*: That's what I've been trying to tell you, Doctor Epstein.

Learn script language.

Whether you are writing a movie, play, TV show, or a graphic novel, there are universal terms when writing a script. Below are some to help you get started:

Close up: Full face of your character. Close ups help you design an exciting page. Often they are pop images such as a close up of an eye, mouth, object, etc.

Cut to: Transition from one scene to another. This helps your graphic novel move rapidly. In the beginning of movies, as credits roll, there may be many "cut to's" to create the mood for the movie.

Establishing shot: General view of area. This usually sets the time, place, and mood of your graphic novel. Many times the splash page is the establishing shot.

Exterior (EXT): Outside view. After several "inside" panels of a room, (even if you show your characters at different angles) the panels may get monotonous. Once you've established who is saying what, then showing an outside view will help break up the monotony. By using balloons with pointers, your characters can be talking from a building, house, or skyscraper for an exciting exterior view.

Flashback: Cuts to a story from a past storyline. It is important to establish your character before he/she/it flashes back.

FX: (sound effects) **POW! CRASH! BANG! KE-POW! POP!** Sound effects are great tools to use for action and to make something pop on your page.

Interior (INT): Inside room, house, hallway, etc.

Long shot (LS): At a distance. It can be medium or extreme. When you design your pages, you may be showing many long shots to create movement on your page.

Over the shoulder: Camera is looking into the face of the other character from the first character's vantage.

Point of view (POV): A scene is seen from one character's perspective.

Have a go-to person.

It helps if you know somebody like your character. It could be a friend, somebody on television, in the movies, or it could be a combination of several people. Don't be surprised when you go to your go-to character, if he/she/it gives you just the dialogue you've been looking for. If your character is you or has characteristics like yours, then *you* are your go-to person.

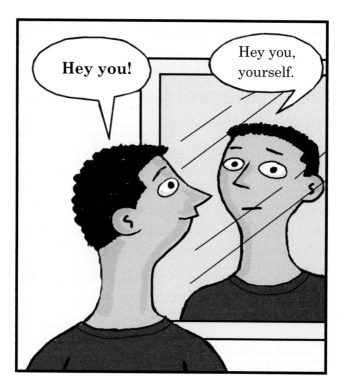

Changing your bible and plotline is part of your process.

As you progress in your story, you will most likely get to know things about your character that you didn't know in the beginning. Maybe some personality trait you *thought* your character had, he/she/it doesn't have at all. Or maybe an action that you *thought* was part of your character's personality is not the way your character would act in the end. Going back to your bible or plotline to change or add something is part of your creative process. Embrace it. It will make your story better.

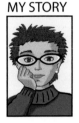

Dialogue is Everywhere!

"Truth is stranger than fiction" has become a cliche because it is so true. You never know what you are going to see or hear that will inspire you. All you have to do is keep your eyes and ears open! I got some of my best characters from overhearing (okay, eavesdropping) real conversations.

I eavesdropped my way through three graphic novels for Marvel Comics.

Several years ago, Tom DeFalco, the legendary editor-in-chief of Marvel Comics, asked me to write a humorous graphic novel for young people about life in the city. It was a dream job! I lived in New York City, it was the '90s, and the Yuppie World was right outside my door. ("Yuppie" is short for Young Urban Professional. This group thinks mostly about themselves, money, and impressing their friends.)

I listened in movie lines, restaurants, bathrooms, and Central Park. (I'm not suggesting that you strain your neck in a restaurant so you are practically sharing a table with total strangers! That is just plain rude!) Be discreet when you listen in!

Even though I tell you to never leave home without a pencil and paper, sometimes I don't follow my own advice. In times like that, I write on napkins, scraps of paper, checks, and even toilet paper! Then I throw everything into my Idea Box and when it's filled to the brim, I begin writing my story.

Here is one of my favorite lines that I wrote on a napkin …

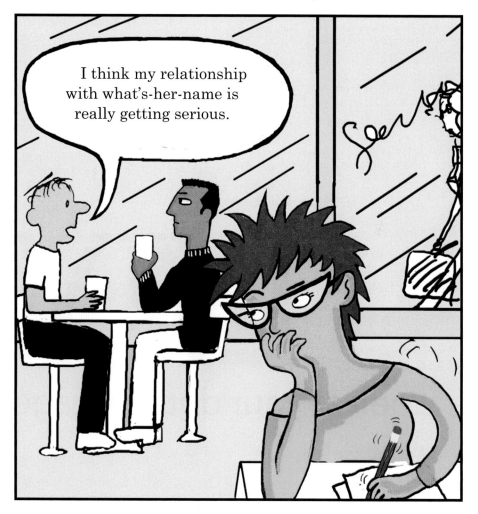

Imagine a guy who thinks he might be getting involved in a serious relationship and he can't even remember the girl's name?

From that one line, I created one of the main characters for my graphic novel about Yuppies—a self-centered guy who is terrified of commitment. And to create conflict, I made up his "what's her-name." She is Julie, a girl who is desperate for commitment. And what a pair they made.

LAY
Look at your double-page

CHAPTER EIGHT

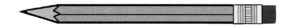

OUT

spread as a giant canvas.

Layout Language

Before you do a layout, it is important to speak the language. It will help you **communicate** your work. Below are the ABCs of layout language.

This is a **panel.** It can be any size or shape. Each panel moves your story forward.

These are **dialogue balloons.** Use them to show your characters talking.

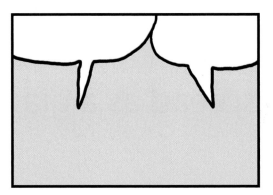

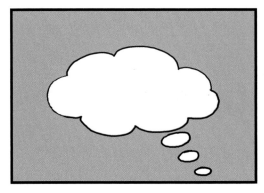

This is a **thought balloon.** It tells you when your character is thinking to him/her/itself.

Your character is whispering.

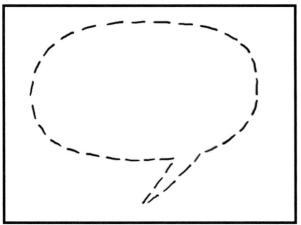

Your character is shouting!

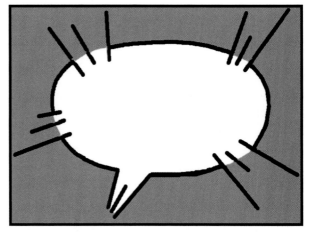

Improvise! You can express emotion in many ways. (Check out graphic novels to see how your favorite artists do it.)

Your dialogue balloons, thought balloons, and other shapes are all part of your layout. You can draw the most amazing art, but if the balloons are not included as part of your design, then your reader will be distracted. They should not be squeezed into your panel as an afterthought. *Practice drawing and placing balloons.* They will give your layout a clean and cohesive look.

LEFT TO RIGHT

The traditional American readers read from left to right. On a typical comic book page, your page may have six panels. (Some pages only have one panel while other pages have as many as twenty!)

These panels are read consecutively (one right after the other) or in a sequence. Graphic novels and comic book art is often called sequential art.

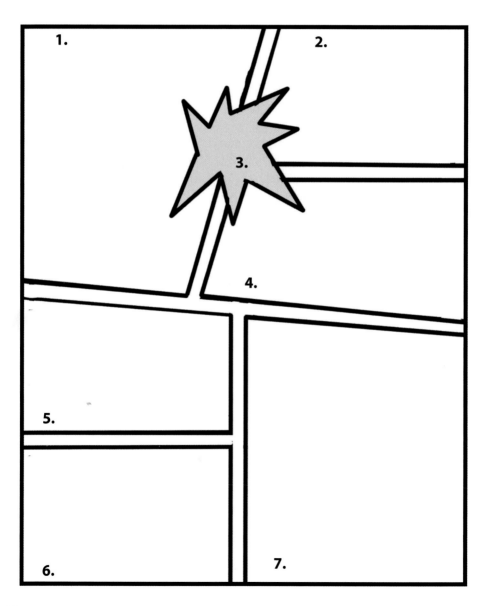

RIGHT TO LEFT

Manga (Japanese comic books) is read from the right side to the left, opposite of traditional American books. Not only do you read the panels from right to left, but you also open the book from the opposite direction of the traditional American style.

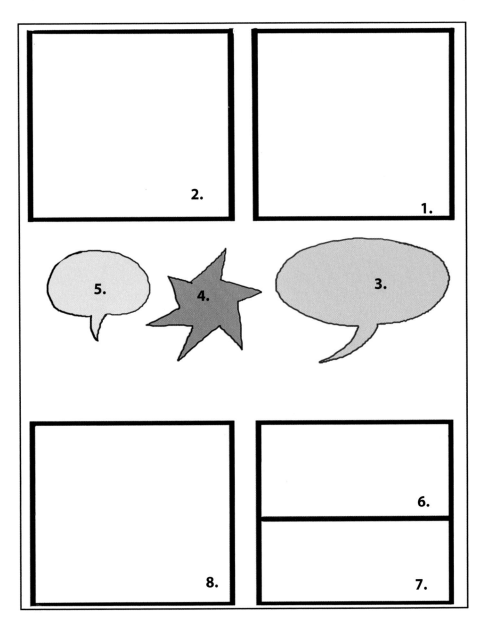

Doing Layouts

Whether you are writing about superheroes, romance, horror, fantasy, or your life, *every page is a new adventure because every page is different.*

It is not unusual to spend hours with a pencil and a pad of paper to get a good layout. (You may want to buy newsprint paper to sketch your layouts. Newsprint is fun to draw on and not expensive.) Doing a good layout combines all your skills of writing, drawing, character development, and plotting.

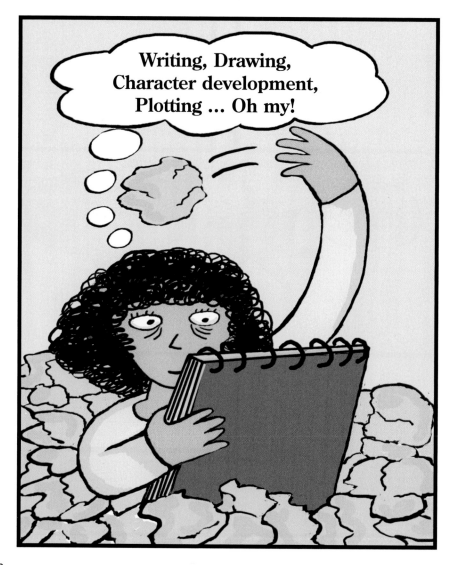

"You are the camera."
Draw an interior shot …
then an exterior one.
Close up … pull back.
Try different angles.
Make something **pop!**

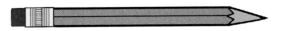

First Impression

Your reader will get an overall first impression of your layout. Although he/she will read one panel at a time, the eye naturally takes in the whole spread. *Your layout should capture your reader's imagination.*

Don't crowd too much information on your double-page spread. Your pages should be visually pleasing with your panels in consecutive order. If your panels are arranged haphazardly and your eye cannot follow which panel comes next, then you will have a confused reader.

There are no shortcuts. To do a successful layout, you will need a clear understanding of what you want to accomplish on your double-page spread. Ask yourself, *"What is it I want to achieve?"* Visualize your beginning and ending panels. Once you know where you want to start and where you want to end on your page, then it is easier to figure out what goes in the middle.

Draw quick sketches. Keep your pencil moving. Get down as much information as you can. A finished panel (or close to being finished) is too big a commitment when you are just beginning your layout.

If it is difficult for you to draw quick sketches, then *switch hands.* You will be operating from the opposite side of your brain. When you switch back to your other hand, you will feel freer. You are ready to tighten (make clearer) your sketches when your eye can move easily across your page.

Look at your favorite graphic novels. What about the layout grabs your attention? Is it the writing, the art, characters, plotline, or all of them?

Each panel stands **alone** as a work of art **and** works in harmony with all the other panels on your double-page spread.

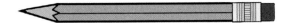

Layout Tips

Number your pages.

It's not just in comic book stories that a wind comes sweeping along, blowing your pages everywhere! It happens in real life, too. Numbering your pages will help you put your story back together again. It also serves as a point of reference when you give your graphic novel to somebody to read for feedback.

Study the layouts of your favorite graphic novelists.

What is it about their pages that catches your eye? Did you ever pick up a graphic novel in a book store and open one page and then put it back on the shelf? If you did, it was probably because the art did not grab you. You can write the greatest story ever told but if your page is not visually exciting, then you will probably lose a reader.

Make a big splash!

The splash page has to grab your reader's attention so your reader will want to know what happens next. It often introduces your main character, shows the setting (the time and place of your story), and has your name and the title of your graphic novel on it.

Dialogue balloons are part of your art.

Do not throw them in as an after thought. Placement of your dialogue balloons is not only important to your storyline, but also to your artwork. Messy balloons can be a distraction from your art.

Try not reading.

When doing a good layout, you should be able to look at your art and get the idea of your story without reading a single word.

Use angles.

Angles are the position or attitude that shows how something is viewed. Remember, *you* are the camera. By using different viewpoints, or angles, you can keep the panels on your double-page spread exciting.

There are many angles to choose from. You can choose a side-angle (when you view your character from the side), or a bird's eye view (looking down like a bird in a tree), or a worm's eye view (looking up from the ground like a worm). You can choose an over-the-shoulder view, a front view, or a three quarter view. Whatever angles you use, keep your panels moving.

Talking heads get boring very quickly.

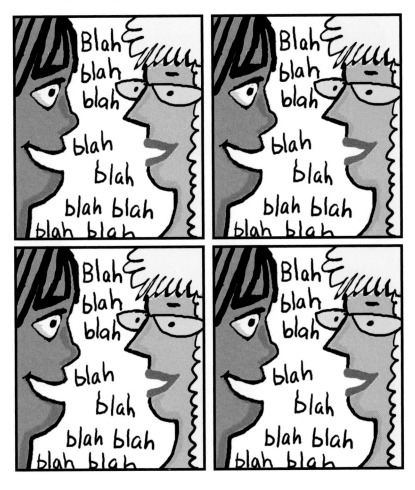

Make something pop on your page.

It's the first thing your reader's eye will go to. Use an everyday object, or a close up of an eye, mouth, or hand.

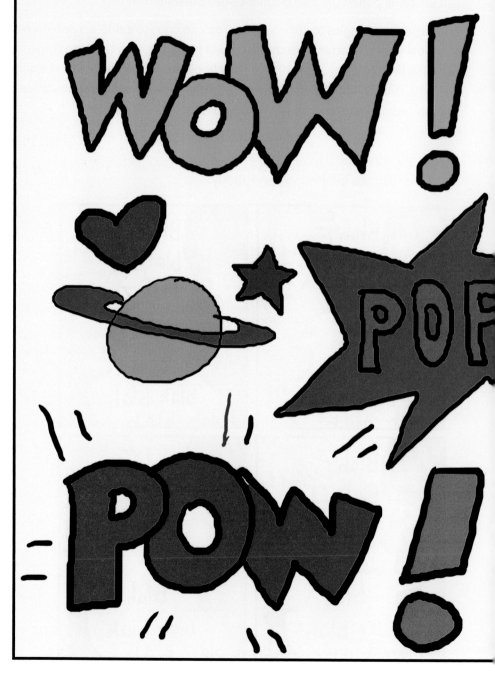

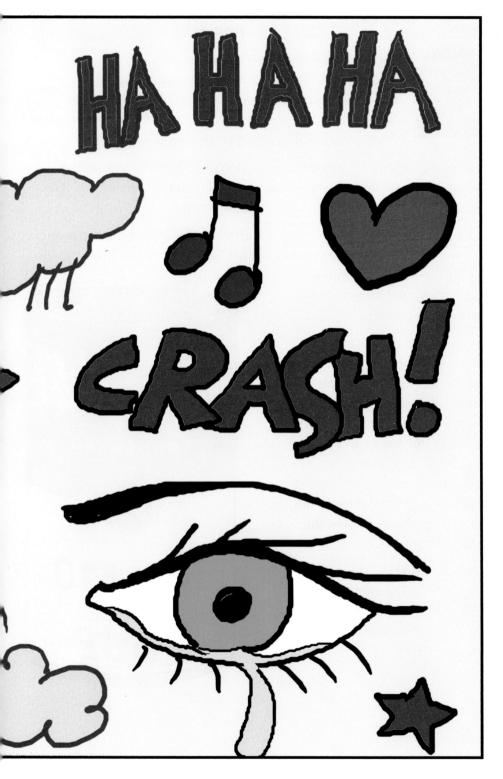

Pop Art

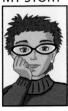

Pop Art comes from the word "popular." Andy Warhol, my favorite artist, was one of the first American Pop Artists. He took everyday popular items such as Campbell's Chicken Soup cans and Brillo boxes and painted them on canvas. Andy Warhol thought everything was art, even soup cans!

Before Pop Art, the Art World was exploding with *Abstract Expressionism,* which dealt with feeling, emotion, and paint dripping on canvas. And then POW! The Pop Art Movement burst onto the scene.

One summer, I was talking to Henry Geldzahler, Modernist art historian and curator of the Metropolitan Museum of Art. He was known as "the eye of the twentieth century" and I always felt it was an honor to be in his presence.

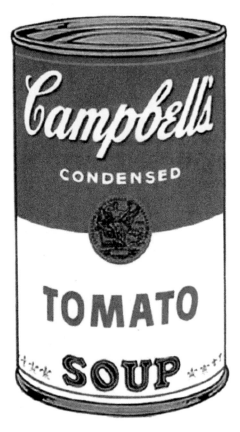

On that bright summer day, Henry told me the story about when Andy showed him his first canvas of a soup can. It had dripping paint. Henry asked why the drip and Andy, knowing that Abstract Expressionist paintings were the rage, replied that every painting drips. Henry encouraged Andy to paint the soup can dripless.

Andy followed Henry's sage advice. The dripless, straightforward, in-your-face can of soup is an icon of the Pop Art movement.

Try different shaped panels.

Triangles, circles, hearts, and octagons can add excitement to your page. Instead of drawing a square or rectangular panel, try mixing it up and drawing your character in a circle or another shape.

Sticky notes are fun to work with. They look like panels and can easily be moved around. They also come in all sizes and shapes and may help to inspire an awesome page.

Feel the push-pull of your page.

You will want your page to come alive by pushing your scenes in and then moving them out. Remember you are the camera.

Art or story ... which comes first?

You decide. Some artists like to lay out their entire graphic novel and then go back and put in the dialogue. Others like to write a detailed script, describing every panel word for word for the artwork. Still others like to lay out their story and write in the dialogue at the same time. Everybody works differently. Figure out what works best for you. *Get to know your process.*

Pretend you are making a movie.

Just like the director is shooting every frame, *you* are deciding every panel. In movie making, not only does the story have to be captivating, but the story has to unfold in a visually exciting way. The same is true with a graphic novel.

Hollywood loves graphic novels! Many graphic novels and comic books have been made into movies. The graphic novel can become the storyboard for the movie. (A storyboard is sequential drawings of the scenes in a movie. They are used in movies, TV shows, soap operas, advertising, etc.)

A Sample Layout

Below is a double-page spread for Archie Comics. It is part of a six page story titled "Betty in The Last Dance." I am the layout artist and writer. I use stick figures to quickly design my page and write notes to the penciller for a clear understanding of what is happening in the panel.

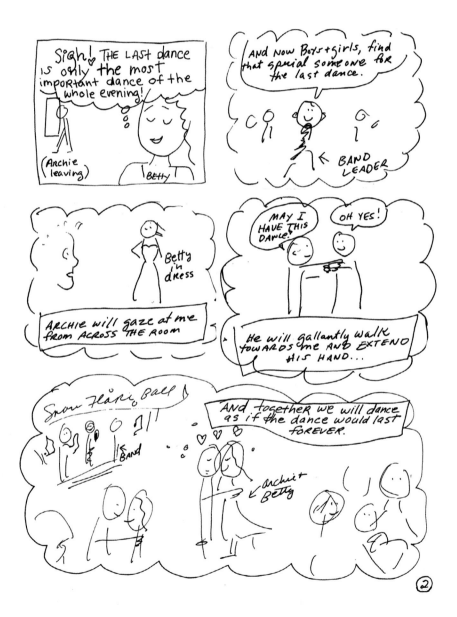

In the first panel, Archie (Betty's love interest) is leaving the store. Betty is wearing the dress she wants to buy. Note that thought balloons are used as entire panels to indicate that Betty is daydreaming. When Betty discovers the dress is too pricey for her budget, she wonders what she's going to do. By figuring out the first and last panels, I can fill in the middle panels to complete my layout.

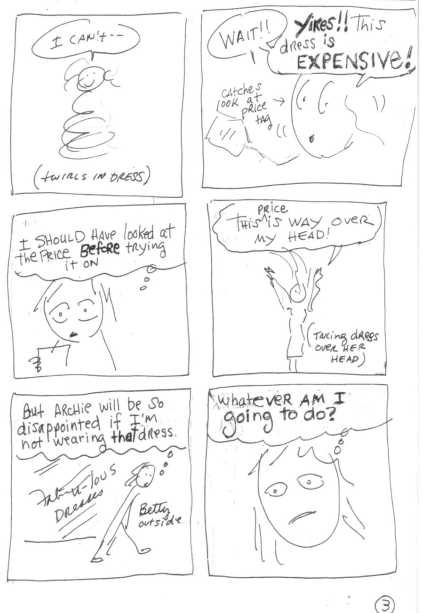

The Pencils

This is the penciled art that the *one and only* Stan Goldberg drew from my sketches and notes on the previous pages.

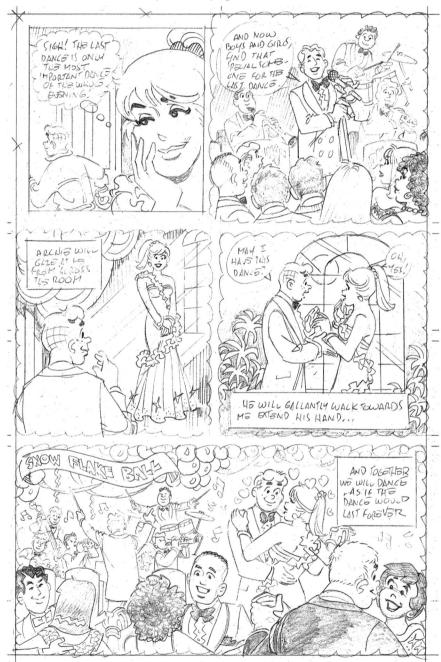

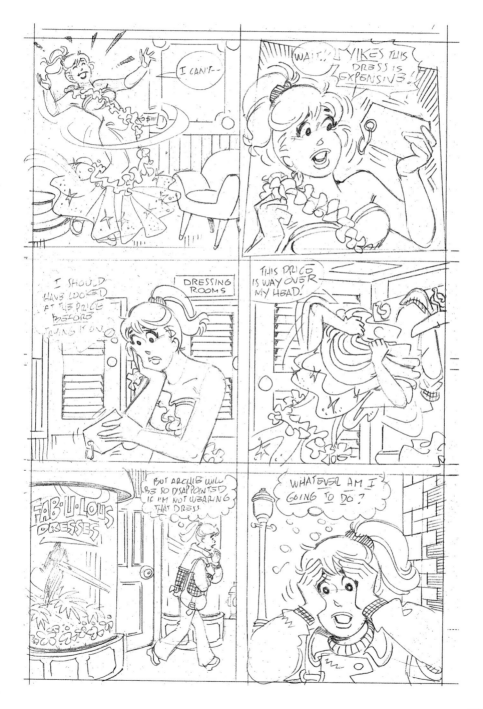

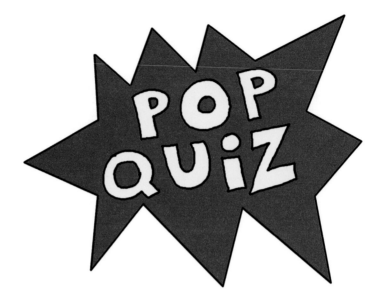

Look at the page you are working on in your graphic novel.
Then answer the questions below:

1. Is your page interesting? Exciting? Is it moving in a consecutive order?

2. Does it work as a double-page spread? A single page? A panel?

3. Is something popping?

If you have answered "yes" to all these questions, then
CONGRATULATIONS!
You are on your way to becoming a great layout artist.

CHAPTER NINE

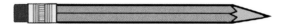

Finishes

Inking, lettering, and coloring

Inking

Did you ever hear the saying, "Different strokes for different folks?" Basically, it means that everybody has a different way of doing things. This saying really rings true when it comes to inking your graphic novel.

Everybody has a different stroke. Inking is when you follow the pencil line with an ink line and adding your own unique style. Some artists use brush and ink, others use one of the hundreds of pens that line the racks of your favorite art supply store, while still others use a croquil pen.

What's Your Line?

The Basics

The Thick and Thin line:

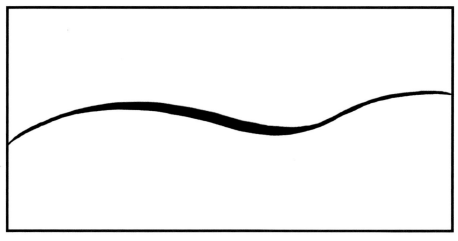

Most of the time, the thick/thin line is achieved with a brush stroke, however, there are several pens that have a brushlike point that will also give you this effect.

Vary your line by applying pressure to the brush or point. It takes a lot of control to master this thick/thin technique but it is well worth it. Your lines will have both character and dimension.

The Consistent line:

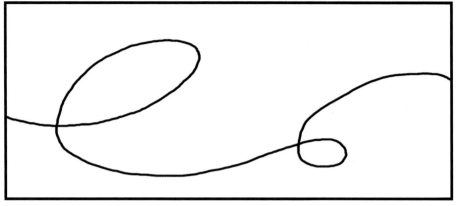

Some artists like a line that is consistent. That is, the line has the same weight throughout your book. This has a nice, neat look to it.

For a consistent line, you will be applying the same amount of pressure on your pen throughout your book. You may need to buy several pens because your tip may get worn out, causing a thicker, inconsistent line.

The Scratchy line:

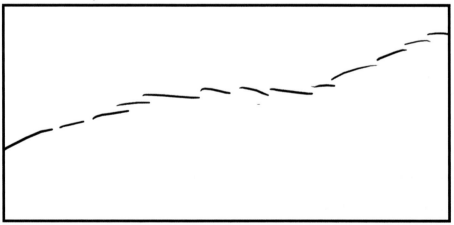

Break it up. Many cartoonists use this line to show action and movement.

The best way to find your line is to *practice, practice, practice.* Once you get the hang of it, you will get into a Zen-like trance and be able to ink page after page of your graphic novel.

Below is the same drawing with three different strokes.

The Thick and Thin line:

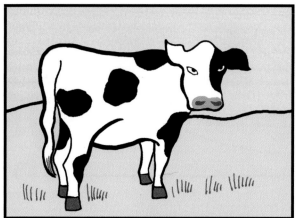

The Consistent line:

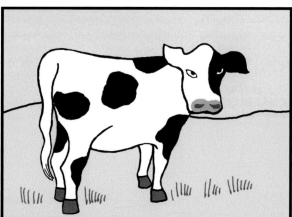

The Scratchy line:

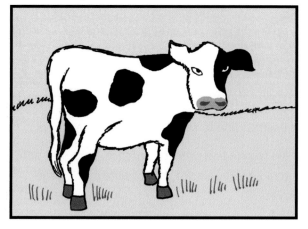

Which one do you like best? Which is closest to your style of inking? Or is your style none of the above?

The Classic

The croquil pen and the ink bottle are classics. Many of the old-timer inking pros, and the ones who have lasted the longest in the industry, use the croquil pen and ink. By using this method, you will achieve beautiful bold black lines with solid black areas.

It takes a lot of practice to get the lines under control. There will probably be lots of splatters. But once you get the hang of it, all the practice will be well worth it.

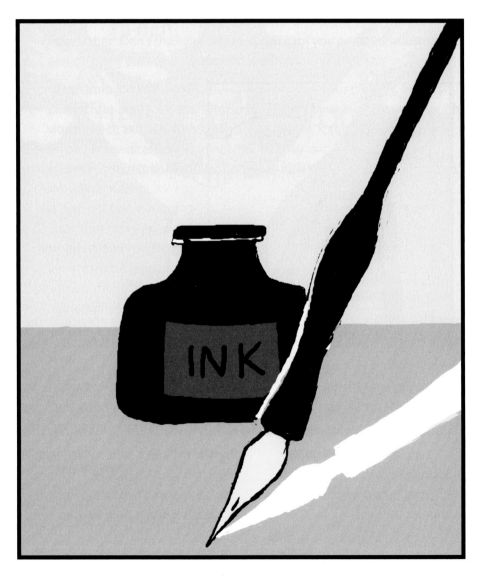

The Penciller and the Inker

Inking can be very intimidating because when you use ink, it is final. Before you begin, make copies of your pencil drawings. That way you will have a clean copy if you don't like the inking and want to start all over again.

Some of the biggest battles in comic book history are between the inker and penciller. The penciller has just spent hundreds of hours drawing pages—every line crafted with love, passion, and angst. Then the penciller has to hand his "babies"*(pages)* off to the inker who can either enhance or destroy them.

On the other hand, sometimes the penciller's lines are difficult to follow. They may be too light, or unfinished, or sloppy.

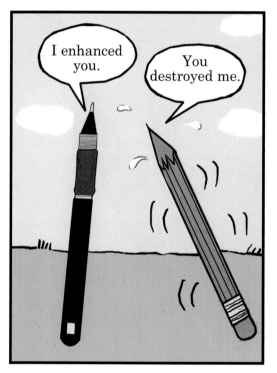

The inker not only has to create a beautiful inked page, but also has to interpret the penciller's lines. If you have really clean pencil lines, you may scan your pages into a computer and tap, tap, tap a few keys and turn your pencil lines into an ink line. It's "Image, Adjustments, Threshold" on my computer. Yours may be different.

Although you will have ink lines to work with, you will probably need to go over some of your lines and add your black areas.

Using Your Blacks and Whites

Many graphic novels are done in black and white. If you are doing your graphic novel in black and white, make sure you have strong blacks in your drawings. Too much white space will make your page look dull and flat.

There is nothing that makes a panel pop more than a black background.

Before black background …

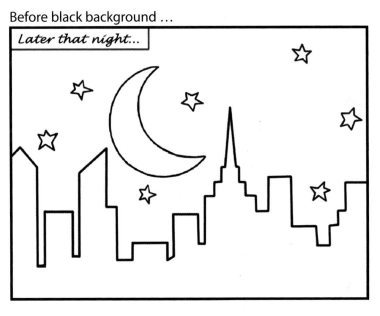

After black background …

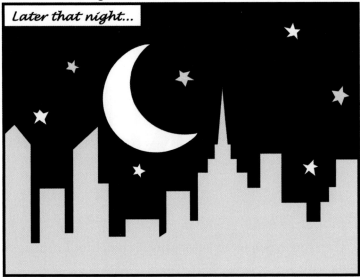

Lettering

The advantage of using your own handwriting is that it is your unique style. Be sure that your letters are big enough so it can be read easily. Do not make it difficult for somebody to read your work. Anytime your reader has to stop to decipher your art or words, it is distracting, annoying, and unprofessional. *Write slowly and neatly.* Try to keep your letters on a straight line. (A ruler may help.) However, if you are one of many artists who shouts …

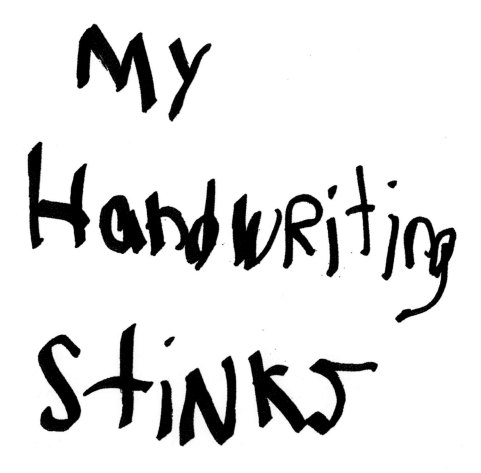

… then you may want to letter using a computer. Choose a **font.** A font is a letter style.

Choosing the Right Font

Lettering is part of your layout. If you are computer lettering, you can choose from hundreds of different styles of fonts. (If you do not own a computer, you can use one at your local library.) Choose a font that is compatible with your cast of characters. It must be easy to read. Too many curlicues or squiggles gets distracting.

There are many books on lettering that can help you select the right font. Go through the fonts and see if any of them jump out at you. (They will not *literally* jump out but it may seem that way!) The more you look at and study different types of lettering, the more you train your eye to select the one that is right for your graphic novel.

If you are writing a gothic story, a typeface like Old English might catch your eye.

For a graphic novel that is funny and all your characters are cartoons, you might want to use Comic Sans.

A spooky story? Your right font may be Chiller.

A romantic tale will look lovely with Lucida Calligraphy.

You might decide to choose a different font for each of your characters. Try to choose the one that represents your creation. If your character is a plus-size girl, she would look silly with tall skinny lettering. On the other hand, a tall, skinny woman would look out of place with big bold letters. When you find the right font, it will feel *font*astic!

Once you have decided your lettering style, scan in your pages and type in your dialogue. If you are drawing on a computer, then you may not need to scan your pages. Make sure to give your dialogue balloons plenty of white space around your lettering. *Arrange and rearrange.* And don't forget to spell check!

Coloring

If you decide to color your book, then you will need to know how. The best way to study coloring is to look. Luckily the world is in full color.

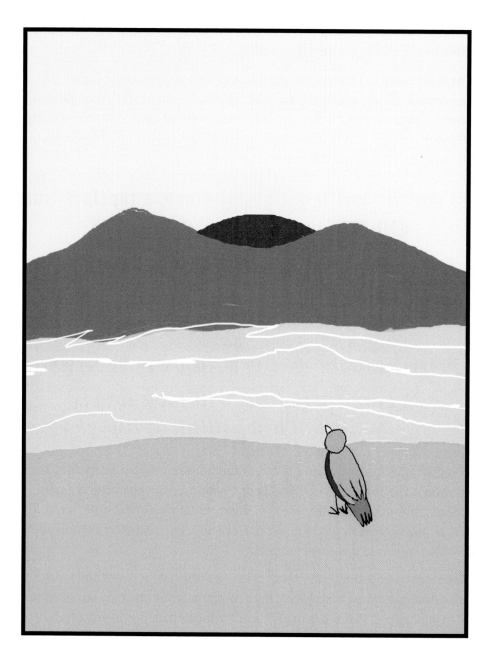

What color is the sky? If you answered "blue" you of course would be right, but how many different shades of blue? A hundred? A thousand? The answer is there are so many shades of blue that it is impossible to count! But if you think the sky is only blue, then look again. The sky is also pink and orange and white and yellow. Have you ever seen a purple sky? Start really looking and see all the different colors of the sky. Also look to see how color changes under light and shadow; day and night; and summer, winter, fall, and spring.

Coloring helps your comic book or graphic novel become a finished work of art. Studying the coloring style from your favorite graphic novels and comic books is very helpful. Look how the pros handle color, lighting, and shading. There are also many books about color theory that you can borrow from your local library.

You may want to color on a computer. There are so many programs to choose from. Find one that works for you. I like Adobe Photoshop. Once you scan in your page, you can practice your coloring skills. If you start by coloring in your background, you will probably use colors that recede (move back or away). Purple, blue, and green recede into the background, while red, orange, and pink advance (come forward) on your page. Keep looking until you train your eye to see what colors advance and which recede.

Color in what you know. If you are doing a superhero and your hero always wears a red cape, yellow tights, and a black mask, then you have a place to start. After you finish your hero's costume, take a look at what is left on your page. It is a lot easier to finish coloring your page once you get started.

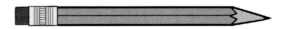

The Final Result!

Here are the finished pages from "Betty in The Last Dance."

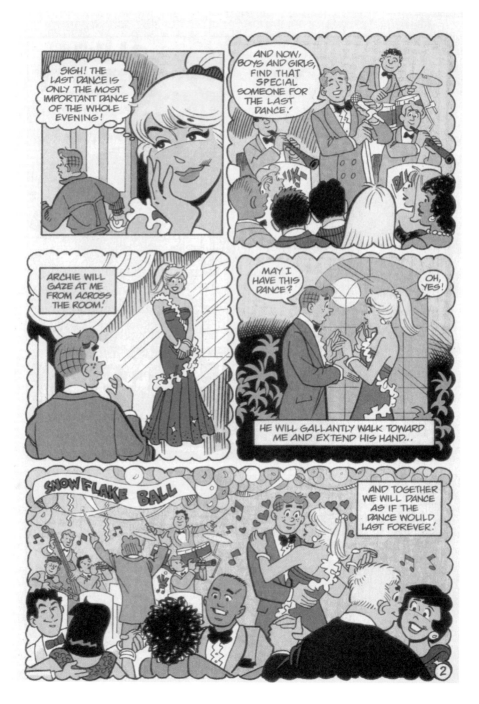

Writer: Barbara Slate; Pencils: Stan Goldberg; Inks: Jon Lowe; Letters: Vickie Williams; Colors: Barry Grossman; Editing: Victor Gorelick. As you can see, it takes six people to do a typical comic book.

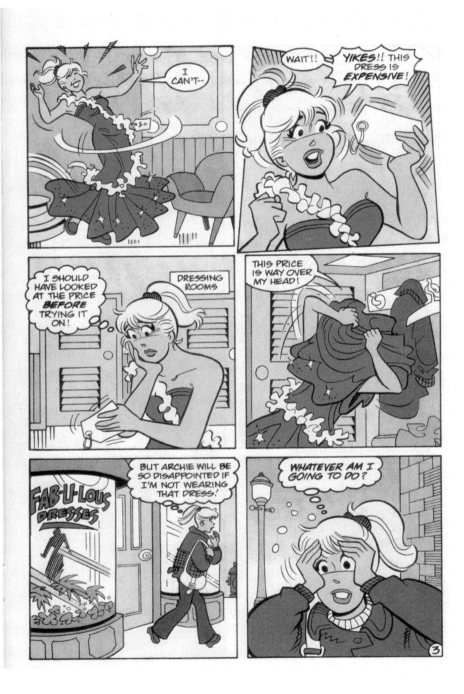

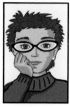

The Perfect Pen

I love pens. I find them irresistible. I have bought hundreds, maybe a thousand, of them and have spent countless hours walking up and down the pen aisle looking for the perfect one. And just when I think I have finally found perfection, another even more enticing pen appears on the rack! Maybe there is no such thing as the perfect pen, but here are three *musts* ...

It must be comfortable in your hand.

Try the one with a soft rubber material around the grip. With this soft material, you can avoid the deep crease in your knuckle. It also helps to keep your hand from cramping after hours of work.

It must have a smooth flowing line.

I like to bring a swatch of the paper I am using for my graphic novel. You may love the flow of the line when you sample it at the store, but when you get home, it may not have that same fluidity on your paper.

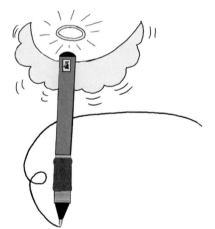

The ink must be permanent.

My entire nine issues of *Angel Love* (about 250 pages) was inked with a nonpermanent pen. Leave the pages in sunlight and day by day the image disappears until all that is left is a blue nonreproductive line. I keep my remaining *Angel Love* pages stored in a box, never to see the light of day. That was a tough lesson, but one I learned well.

CHAPTER TEN

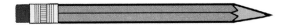

Some Students' Work

Angelica Speer, age 14 *Venom's Antidote*

Patrick Henneberry, age 12 *Spirit War*

Gabriel Constantine, age 14 *The Hidden*

Nicole Shedrick, age 15 *Just B-4 Midnight*

Katherine J. Devereux-Smith, age 14 *Project Crow*

Jack Quattrochi, age 13 *Memories*

by Angelica Speer, age 14

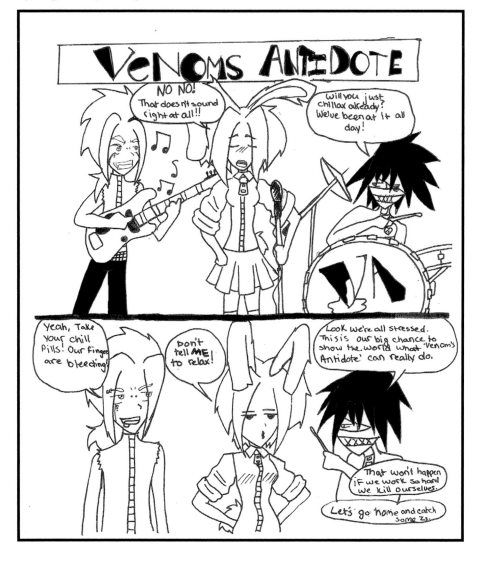

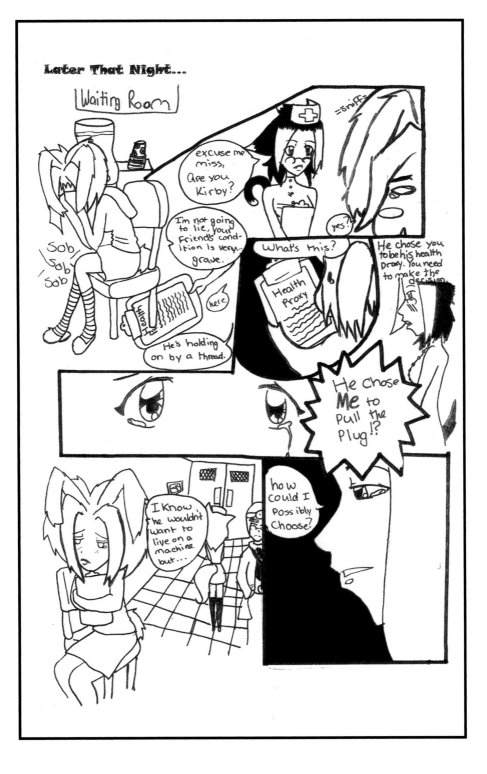

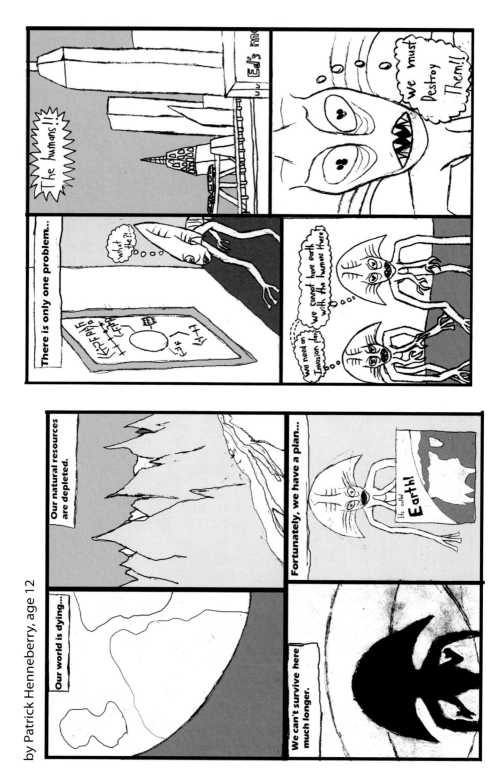

by Patrick Henneberry, age 12

150

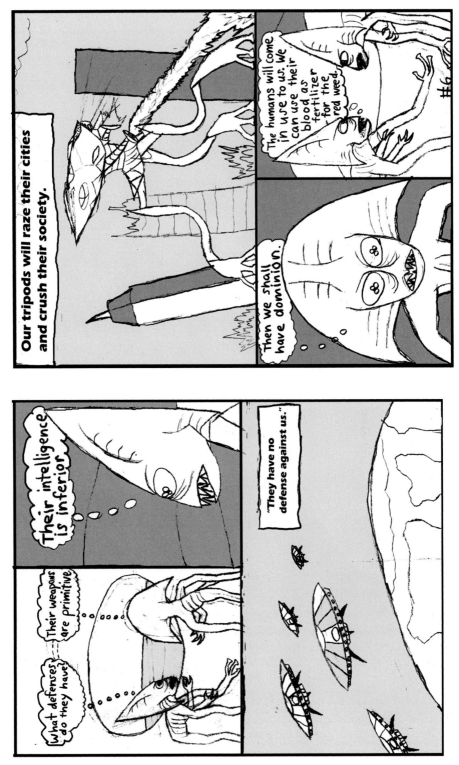

151

by Gabriel Constantine, age 14

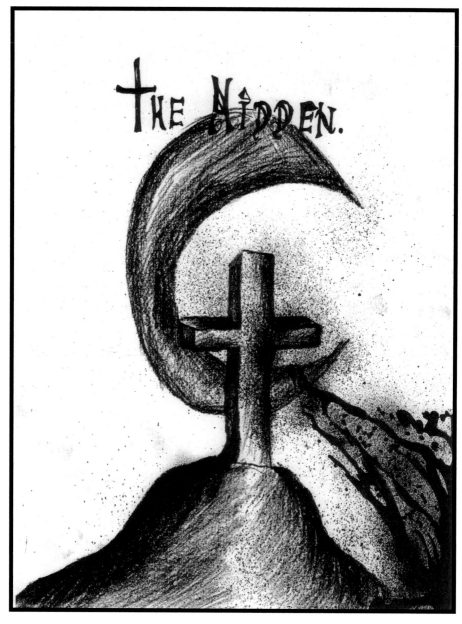

152

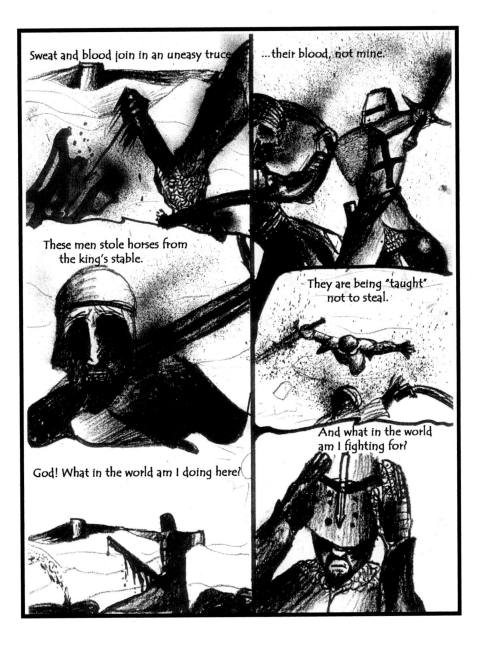

by Nicole Shedrick, age 15

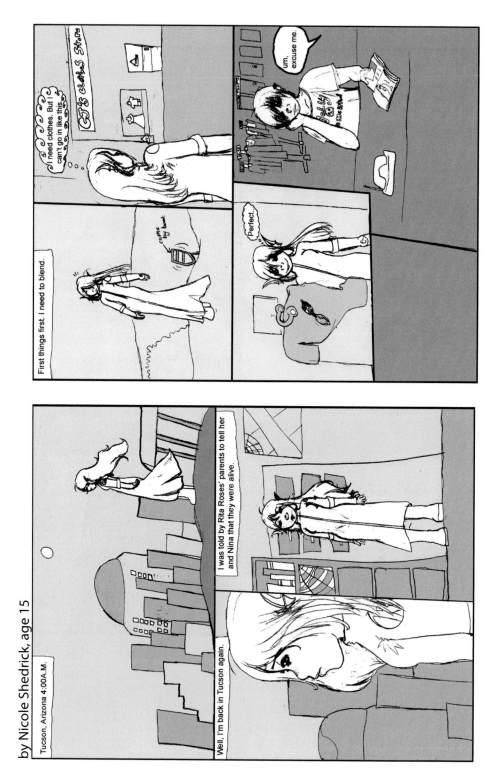

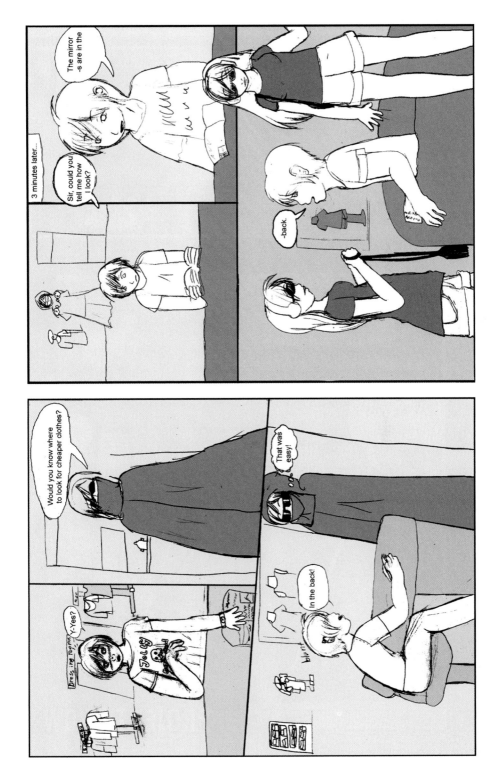

155

by Katherine J. Devereux-Smith, age 14

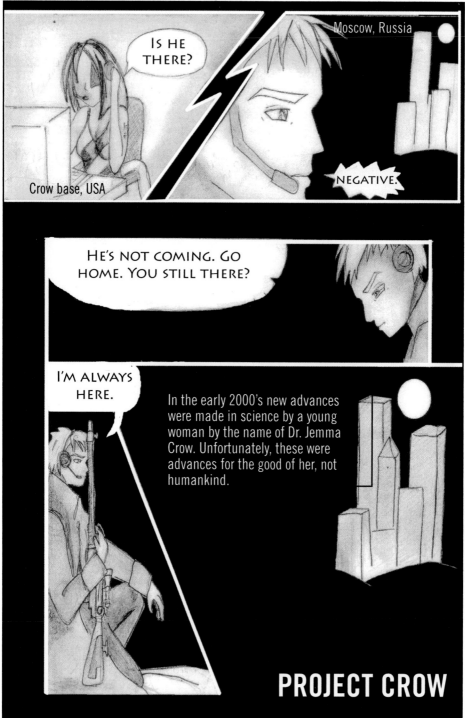

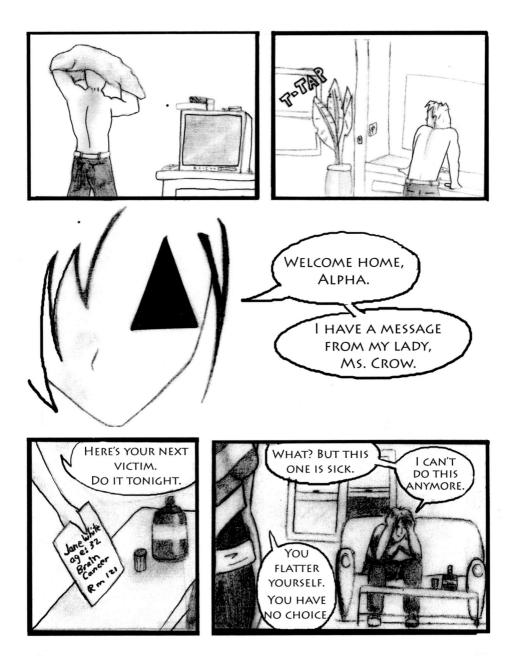

by Jack Quattrochi, age 13

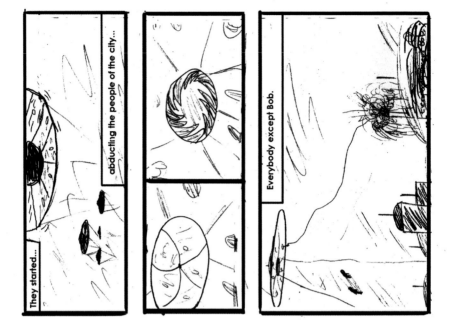

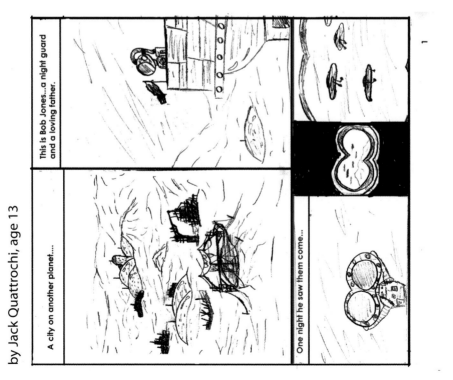

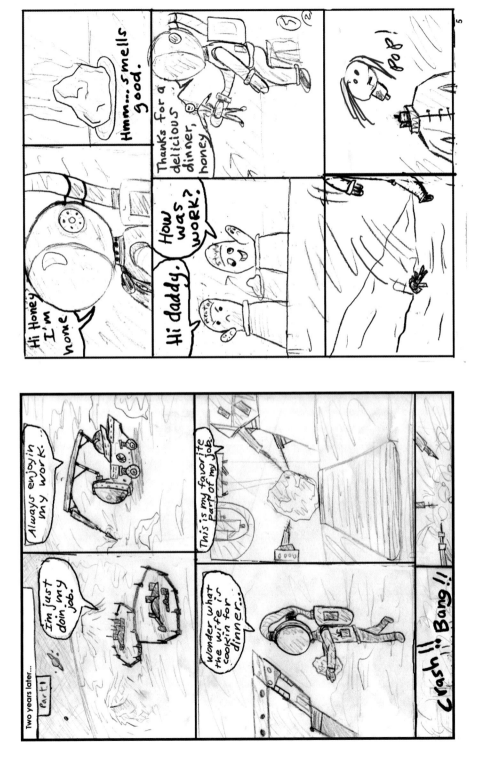

159

The

If you are not connected ...

CHAPTER ELEVEN

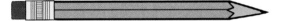

"Biz"

… then get connected.

A **contact**

is somebody who knows somebody who knows somebody who has a distant cousin who works at your dream job and is willing to get **you** in the door.

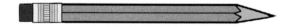

Opportunities often happen through **contacts.** But if you are like most people who know nobody (at least nobody who you think can help advance your career), then you have to make your own connections. It may surprise you that getting connected can start right in your own neighborhood.

Ways To Connect

Take art classes.

You may find art classes at your local library, community center, or museums. There, you can meet other artists and get feedback on your work. If you are in high school, ask your art teacher if you can spend more time in the art room either after school or during your free periods. Talk to your guidance counselor about which art schools have a good graphic novel program. It's never too early to plan for your future.

Check out interactive websites.

If you don't have a computer, then use one at your local library. Many comic companies have interactive websites. You can submit your pages to online contests. You just might win! (Make sure you are submitting your work to honorable companies.) Many up-and-coming graphic novelists have made good contacts through these contests. It is also a good way to see what other artists/writers are doing.

Visit museums.

Learn from the masters! Go to a museum as often as possible. The more works of art you look at, the better your eye will see. Go back and look at paintings that you have studied before. Look at them *as if for the first time.* Do you see something new? Something that you have never seen before?

Network.

Networking is talking to people with the hope of advancing your career. Always keep your eyes and ears open for a good opportunity. Many artist/writers would rather sit in their studios and work on their graphic novels than go out into the world. Working hard is important, but so is connecting with people.

Talk to your teacher, counselor, other artists, or anybody else who can give you good advice. People love helping talented and motivated artist/writers! It gives them bragging rights when your first graphic novel is published.

Make eye contact.

It is important to look the person who you want to connect with in the eye. When you look somebody in the eye, you have a better chance at being remembered than if you look away or at the floor or ceiling. If you are really shy, practice making eye contact with a friend or family member.

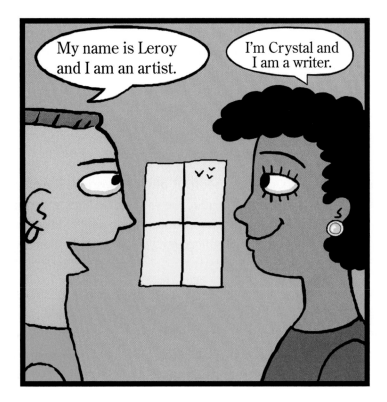

Visit your local library.

Most librarians are excellent listeners and enjoy helping aspiring graphic novelists. Your librarian may connect you to interesting events that are happening either at the library or in your community.

Do not be shy about talking to your librarian.

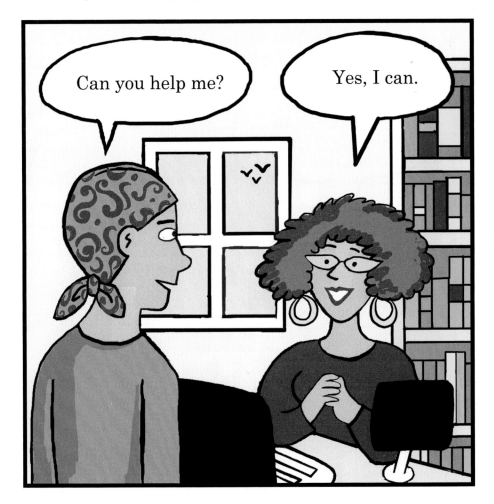

Your librarian may be planning a signing of a famous writer, or sponsoring a course by a professional on how to do graphic novels. Many libraries sponsor Anime movies (Japanese animation). Attending these Animes will connect you to other artists and writers. *You never know who you will meet!* You may even meet the perfect artist or writer to collaborate with you on your graphic novel.

Many libraries have an entire section dedicated to graphic novels. By spending time in the Graphic Novel section, you can read and study all different styles of art and storytelling. It is always good to keep up with what other artists/writers are doing. *Know your business.*

Your librarian might recommend a book for you to read that is just what you need to advance your story.

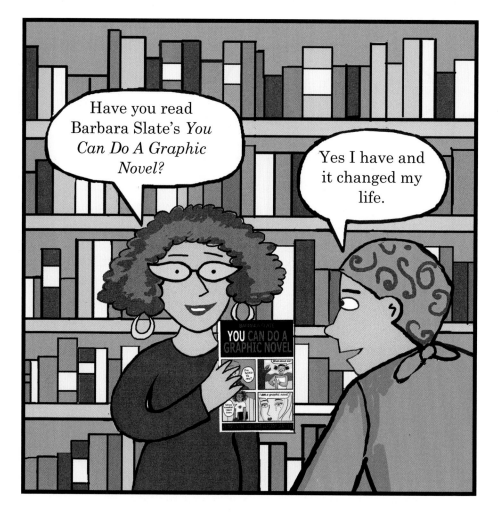

(I know it's tacky to be so blatant about promoting my own book, but the truth is, self-promotion is not a bad thing. As long as you don't clear rooms bragging about your latest brilliant effort, then self-promoting is often the only way to get recognized, especially in the beginning of your career.)

Go to comic book conventions.

Check your local newspaper for comic book conventions in your area. Many artists and writers have gotten their big break that way. (If you ever get the chance, go to the ones in San Diego and New York City. They are the mind-boggling biggies.)

* At a comic convention, the pros give you feedback on your work. It is well worth standing in line to get an objective opinion. *Listen carefully* to what "the Pro" says. It can save you hours, days, and maybe even years of going off in the wrong direction.

* It is a good idea to have a pencil and paper available so you can take notes. Sometimes it's not easy to really listen because you may be nervous about showing your work or you may be awestruck because your favorite writer in the whole world is right in front of you talking to you about your story.

* Walk down Artist Alley to see great artists from everywhere, drawing in every style. They will talk to you and give you terrific tips. You can make great contacts.

* You get to meet creators, artists, and writers. Do not be surprised if your favorite graphic novelist is there.

* The comic conventions are great places to preview the latest Hollywood movie based on a graphic novel. It's really fun to see a movie before it even hits your local theatre.

* Inspiration is everywhere! When you get home from a convention, you will probably have a major breakthrough. *Get to work!*

A good contact will
get you in the door.

The rest is up to you.

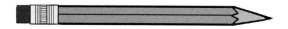

Make a good first impression.

You only get one chance to make a first impression. *Make it a good one.*
Below are three musts:

Be clean.

Be sure to brush your teeth, comb your hair, take a bath or shower, and wear
clean, neat clothes when you go to meet somebody who can help you in
your career.

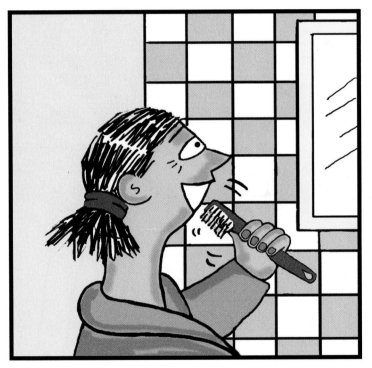

Do not be late.

Nobody likes to be kept waiting, especially somebody who is doing *you* a
favor.

Be a good listener.

Write down three questions you want answered. (Even if you know what
you want to ask, write them down anyway. You may get nervous and forget
a question.) *Don't interrupt.* You will learn more if you listen rather than talk.

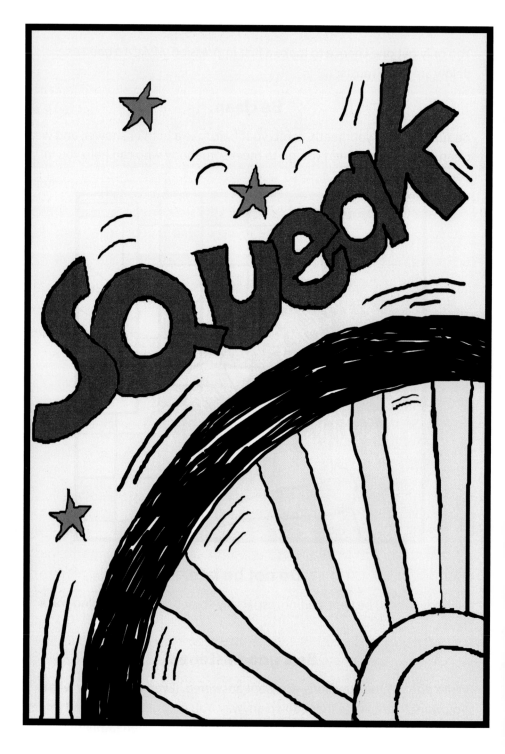

Be the "squeaky wheel."

Did you ever hear the saying, "The squeaky wheel gets the grease?" It means that one wheel is going to get greased while the other ones are not. Usually it's the one making the most noise that gets the grease.

Be the squeaky wheel when you have a good contact. The truth is, many jobs have been found that way. Most good contact people are very busy. That is why *you* make contact. (Constant contact can get annoying. Be careful not to get too squeaky!)

Your contact could be somebody you met at a comic convention, a library event, a museum, or somebody you feel comfortable talking to like a teacher, coach, or guidance counselor. A simple e-mail or dropping a note in the mail is a good way to stay in touch.

I have taught many students and the ones who call occasionally and attend my classes are usually the ones I get in touch with when a good opportunity comes along.

Seize opportunity.

If you get an offer to do any kind of work with a comic book company, a publishing house, a comic book store, or anything that is at all connected to the comic world, seize it! (If you are in school, be sure to talk over your opportunity with a parent, teacher, or guidance counselor.) If it's the real thing, then accept the offer even if you have to sweep floors. Starting at the bottom and working your way up is the best way to break into the business because you will understand all aspects of it. Many comic book legends started this way. Be sure to keep your eyes and ears open for opportunities for advancement and of course, *do a great job!*

You will meet people along the way who will look at your work and if you are talented, they will point you in the right direction. Many people in the comic book world are known for having big hearts.

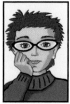

A Nice Gesture Can Change Your Life

Sometimes the work load is so heavy, I have to hire an assistant. When that happens, I usually call the local art school and speak to somebody who writes my information on an index card and then posts it on the bulletin board. The card probably reads something like this …

WANTED:

Assistant to
Comic Book Artist
Must draw well.

Jerry Craft came for an interview. He was nice and I liked his portfolio so I thought I would hire him for the day and see how things worked out. He was talented and easy to work with so we just continued on day after day for over a year. After several months, I told Jerry that I thought it was strange that the art school only sent one applicant. Jerry smiled and said, "It was the flowers." Apparently, the last time he went for an interview, Jerry gave the woman in charge of the bulletin board a bouquet of flowers to thank her for a previous contact. He did not get that job, so when my call came in (and still smelling the flowers) she called Jerry right away. The index card never did get posted on the bulletin board.

Jerry and I worked together every day for over a year. He was courteous, on time, and talented. We are still great friends. Jerry went on to create his own comic strip, *Mama's Boyz,* which is syndicated in many newspapers.

Remember to say …

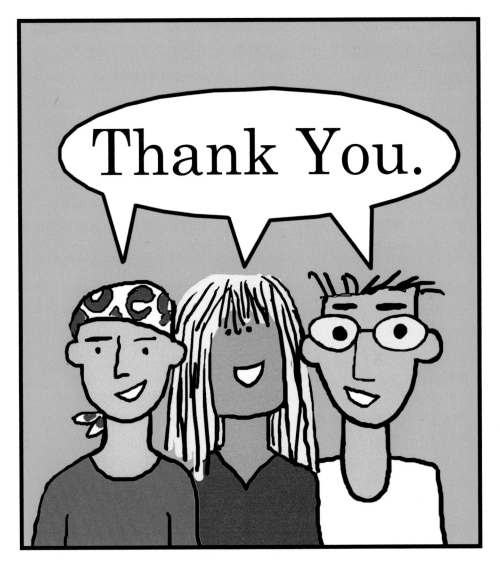

Everybody, no matter how rich or famous, likes to get acknowledged. It can be a teacher, your parents, a contact, a relative, a friend, or an advisor who has inspired or given you good advice. A simple thank you can go a long way. And don't forget to pass on *your* knowledge. It will be a great feeling when somebody says "thank you" to you.

GLOSSARY

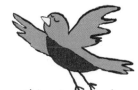

Angle   The position or attitude that shows how something is viewed. Example: A bird's eye view is a view looking down like a bird.

Antagonist   Tries to stop the main character from achieving his/her/its goal. Adversary/Opponent.

Artist's Alley   At many comic book conventions, you can visit awesome Artist's Alley. It is the place where the pros bring their work to show their latest, talk to fans, and work on their pages. You can see how a pro layouts, sketches, and inks.

Background   1. The part of your character that happened before. 2. In a panel, the part of the picture that is toward the back. Usually, a less important position than the foreground.

Bible   Everything you need to know about your characters … and more (name, age, siblings, powers, side-kicks, favorite book, etc.). A full description of your characters so that you know them as well as, or better than, you know yourself.

Biz   (the Biz) Short for "The Business."

Breakthrough   An exhilarating moment when you have struggled hard enough and long enough through your creative process and can suddenly see perfectly clear. A big AHA moment.

Character driven   You create the characters before the story. The art comes first.

Characters   Creations (personalities) that come from your head.

Climax   The moment of highest tension in your story when the conflict comes to a head.

Close up   When writing a script, the direction used to describe a full face of your character. Close ups help you design an exciting page. Often they are pop images such as a close up of an eye, mouth, object, etc.

Collaborate   To work with another person. If you are the artist, you collaborate with a writer. If you are the writer you collaborate with an artist.

Color coding   When plotting, assigning each character a color.

Color palette   The range of colors. Your palette can be from a box of crayons or your computer.

Comic book convention   An inspirational place to go to meet creators and get your work looked at by professionals. A place where graphic novelists and comic books professionals meet and greet.

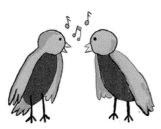

Communicate   Talk. Speaking the same language. To exchange information. 1. Your characters communicate through dialogue to each other. 2. You communicate your story to your reader.

Conflict   The struggle between the Protagonist and the Antagonist.

Consecutive   Panels are laid out one right after the other.

Consistent   The same, compatible. A style of inking in which the line remains the same thickness.

Contact   Somebody who can help you in your career. It can be somebody who knows somebody who knows somebody who has an in at a publishing house. Opportunities often happen through contacts.

Continuity   1. One panel follows another in a clear and logical order, in a continuous way. 2. If your character is wearing a red cape in a panel, unless he/she has changed it, the cape will continue to be red in the next panel. 3. In a "continuity comic strip," it does not have a daily ending or joke. Instead, it continues the next day. Many comic books continue a plotline from month to month.

Creative   Having imagination and ability. Enlightenment, Vision, Muse, Genius.

Creative block   Temporarily prevents you from doing your work. When you suffer from the creative block, you may feel like you will never be able to write or draw again.

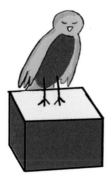

Creative process   Getting to know your creative self and how you work best. Examples: Knowing if you are a morning person or a night owl. Getting to know if you work better with or without music.

Critical voice The voice in your head that causes you to doubt yourself. Usually it is a familiar voice. It may be your own.

Cut to When writing a script, the direction used to describe the transition from one scene to another. This helps your graphic novel move rapidly.

Dialogue Conversation between your characters.

Dialogue balloons Balloonlike shapes that wrap around words to indicate that your character is talking. There is usually a pointer that breaks into the balloon and points to the character who is doing the talking.

Double-page spread Two pages side by side. Look at your double-page spread as a giant canvas.

Edit To arrange, correct, or change your work.

Editor Professional writers and artists have an editor who gives them feedback. An editor can help arrange, correct, and change their work. Depending on the editing, the editor can be loved, hated, and loved and hated at the same time by the author.

Establishing shot When writing a script, the direction used to describe the general view of the area. It usually sets the time, place, and mood of your graphic novel. The establishing shot is often on the splash page.

Evolution Development, change, transformation. The evolution, or how your story evolves, is determined by its highs and lows, twists and turns, plots and subplots.

Exterior (EXT) When writing a script, the direction used to describe an outside view. Many times an exterior panel will be used to break up the monotony of "talking heads."

Falling action   The time in your story after the climax and before the resolution. This usually happens quickly.

Feedback   When somebody reads your graphic novel and offers their opinion.

Finishes   Inking is considered "the finishes" or final phase. However, if you are adding color, that is the last part in completing your graphic novel.

Flashback   When writing a script, the direction used to cut to a story from a past storyline.

Font   A letter style.

Foreground   The front of your panel where the most important action is occurring.

Freedom in your lines   Your pencils or ink lines have a fluid flow. A great compliment!

FX (sound effects) POW! CRASH! BANG! KE-POW! POP!   Great tools to use for action and to make something pop on your page. Used often for fight scenes in superhero comic books.

Getting in the door   A connection that enables you to meet somebody who can help advance your career. It may be an interview for a job. "I don't know if I'll get the job or not, but at least I'm getting in the door."

"Go-to Louie" (go-to person)   Somebody that you know or met or who has left a lasting impression on you that you "go to" in your head to conjure up your character. It can be just one person or a combination of several people. Going there allows you to capture the essence of your character.

Graphic novels   Comic books, only longer. The difference is that a comic book is usually put out in monthly installments. In graphic novel form, the book is complete.

Impression   The way somebody views something. Your reader will have an impression of your work. Much of the time, a "first impression" will determine if the person likes it or not.

Improvise   Creating in the moment. Thinking quickly.

Inking   Following the pencil lines with an ink line. The last, or final phase of your graphic novel.

Inspiration   A sudden bright idea. Genius, Muse, Enlightenment, Brainstorm, Illumination.

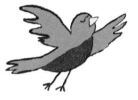

Interior (INT)   When writing a script, the direction used to describe inside room, house, hallway, etc.

Journal   A daily record about the one and only you.

Layout   The way your art is designed on your page to tell your story.

Long shot (LS)   When writing a script, the direction used to describe a distant viewpoint. It can be a medium or extreme distance.

Main plot   The beginning, middle, end, and twist of your story. It is what your story is about.

Manga   Japanese comic books.

Morph   Become something else. In comic books, many ordinary characters morph into something fantastic and become superheroes.

Motto   Creed, mantra, words that you live by. Example: Practice what you preach.

Over the shoulder   When writing a script, the direction used to describe looking into the face of the other character from the first character's point of view.

Pacing   The way your story moves.

Panel   The boxes used in graphic novels or comic books that tell the story.

Permanent ink   Ink that will not fade.

Plot   The way the story unfolds and resolves.

Plotline   Shows the evolution of your story. All its twists and turns, highs and lows, plots and subplots.

Point of View (POV)   When writing a script, the direction used to describe a scene as seen from one character's perspective.

Protagonist   The main character in the story. The one your reader cares about.

Push/pull   When you do a layout, your page comes alive by pushing your camera in for a close up and pulling it back for a long shot. If you study your page, you can feel the push/pull.

Resolution   The point when the conflict is wrapped up. This occurs after the falling action and before the end.

Rising action   The central part of your story where the main conflict (problem) of your characters is developed. This is the build-up of your story. This is where the suspense, drama, or comedy (it can be all of them!) develop to create your successful story.

Sequential art   Another name for graphic novels. The order in which the panels follow one another, one right after the other.

Setting   The time and place of your story.

Sketches   Quick drawings. Drawings in a sketchbook or at the beginning of your layout to design your pages.

Splash page   Often the first page of your comic book or graphic novel. Many times, the splash page is one full page or even a double-page spread.

Story driven   You create the story before the art. The story comes first.

Subconscious   Existing in the mind when much of the time the mind doesn't even know it's there. The part of the mind where many feelings, wishes, and desires are stored.

Subplots   Secondary storyline. In comic books, subplots can become main plots as the comic series progresses.

Talking heads   A term used to describe panel after panel of characters talking with nothing to break the monotony.

Theme   The underlying idea of what your story is really about. Examples: Love conquers all. Honesty is the best policy.

Thought balloons   Cloudlike shapes that show your character is thinking to him/her/itself.

Twist   Every story has a beginning, middle, end, and twist. The twist is the surprise, the unexpected.

Working title   A title of your graphic novel that works for the time being. It may or may not be your final title.

The

End.

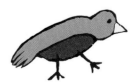

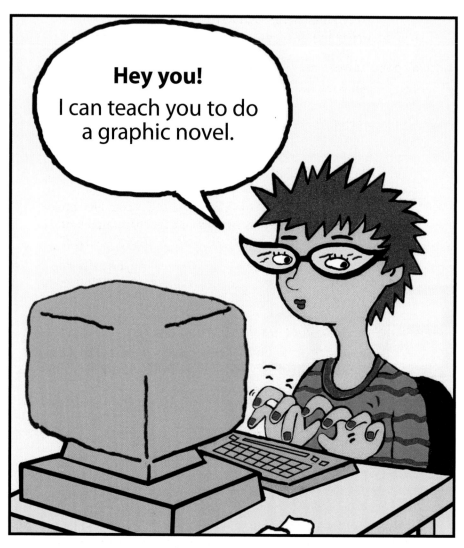

You can have a one-on-one online workshop.

Take an online course. Whether you are a beginner or advanced in your graphic novel, Barbara will personally review and critique your work.

For information: youcandoagraphicnovel.com

Schedule a workshop or lecture
at your local library, school, or art center.

Barbara's popular workshops are tailored for all age groups and levels of achievement. Visit youcandoagraphicnovel.com to learn more.

Praise for Barbara's Workshops

"Wow!!! What an impressive workshop you led for the children today. Your presentation was fabulous! The students were mesmerized by the information you shared, by your life experiences, by your knowledge, and by your expertise and talents. Thank you so very much for being a role model for the kids."

Virginia Peterson,
6th grade English teacher

"Barbara is a dynamic drawing dynamo. She connects with kids and they respond through their art. She knows how to jump-start their creative process to produce stunning results. Teens loved her and her workshop. No one wanted it to end!"

Carol Roberts, Librarian

"I definitely enjoyed the workshop. Before I thought of cartooning as a difficult, almost impossible writing and drawing process, but Barbara made the steps so clear it made creating cartoons possible. I liked working with so many intelligent and talented participants. Since I am home schooled, I found it motivating to work with Barbara and the class. The exercises she gave us helped me to keep working."

Lillie, Student

"I feel very positive and enthusiastic about the workshop. It has increased Alex's interest in the art form and I see the influence of the workshop in his other artwork as well."

Paul, Parent